Strange
California
Monsters

Michael Newton

Schiffer Publishing Ltd

4880 Lower Valley Road Atglen, Pennsylvania 19310

All photos and text unless otherwise noted are courtesy of the author
Artwork by Bill Rebsamen

Schiffer Books are available at special discounts for bulk purchases
for sales promotions or premiums. Special editions, including per-
sonalized covers, corporate imprints, and excerpts can be created
in large quantities for special needs. For more information contact
the publisher:

Published by Schiffer Publishing Ltd.
4880 Lower Valley Road
Atglen, PA 19310
Phone: (610) 593-1777; Fax: (610) 593-2002
E-mail: Info@schifferbooks.com

For the largest selection of fine reference books
on this and related subjects, please visit our web
site at **www.schifferbooks.com**
We are always looking for people to write books
on new and related subjects. If you have an idea
for a book please contact us at the above address.

This book may be purchased from the publisher.
Include $5.00 for shipping.
Please try your bookstore first.
You may write for a free catalog.

In Europe, Schiffer books are distributed by
Bushwood Books
6 Marksbury Ave.
Kew Gardens
Surrey TW9 4JF England
Phone: 44 (0) 20 8392-8585; Fax: 44 (0) 20 8392-9876
E-mail: info@bushwoodbooks.co.uk
Website: www.bushwoodbooks.co.uk

Designed by RoS
Type set in Batik Regular/New Baskerville BT

ISBN: 978-0-7643-3336-1

Printed in The United States of America

Dedication

For Ray Crowe

Acknowledgments

Thanks to Dinah Roseberry at Schiffer Books for her enthusiasm on this project, and to my wife, Heather, for helping me bring it to life. Thanks also to Dave Frasier at Indiana University for his usual tireless assistance in tracing obscure sources, and to Bill Rebsamen for his unique artwork.

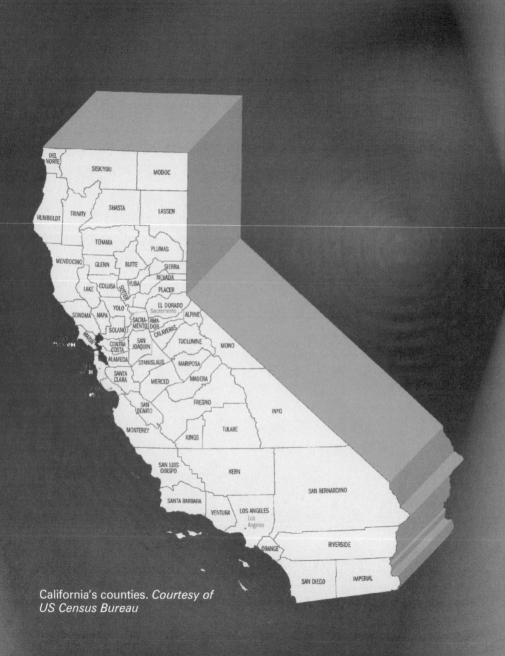

California's counties. *Courtesy of US Census Bureau*

Contents

Seeking Monsters

People love monsters...at a distance.

Since the early 1920s, Americans have spent billions of dollars to watch strange creatures and misshapen humans lurch across movie screens, wreaking bloody havoc. Billions more have been spent to pursue their adventures in print, through novels and pulp magazines. Role-playing games filled with monsters claim legions of fans worldwide.

Monsters are safe, as long as they remain on theater or TV screens, between the covers of a book, or trapped within the alternate reality of games. They cannot reach us there, except in our imaginations.

But what of the other monsters, prowling abroad in real life—gliding through our lakes and oceans, soaring overhead, stalking our forests, lumbering across our highways and invading our own backyards?

What of them?

Before recorded history, humans on every continent, from every culture, feared or worshiped giants, dragons, monstrous beasts of all descriptions. The mythology of every race and nation teems with entities of awesome size and power, alternately used for good or evil, sometimes on a whim.

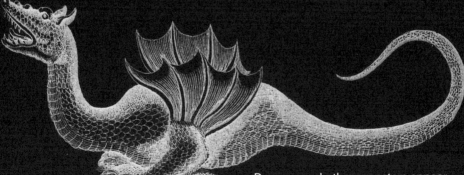

Dragons and other monsters appear in the mythology of all nations.
Courtesy of Michael Newton

Today we recognize that certain monsters of mythology—mermaids, unicorns, some dragons, the many-armed Kraken, even India's dog-sized gold-mining ants—were in fact such mundane beasts as manatees, antelopes, large snakes or lizards, giant squids, and red marmots.[1] Still, others remain unexplained.

The search for monsters—or for creatures of any size and temperament unrecognized by modern science—has a name: *cryptozoology,* defined as the study of "hidden" animals. Various sources claim the term was coined by British naturalist Ivan Sanderson in the 1940s, or by Belgian zoologist Bernard Heuvelmans a decade later.[2]

In either case, the quest did not begin in modern times. Only its name is relatively new. Pursuit of monsters—or "cryptids," as modern researchers prefer to call them, eliminating the negative context and broadening the search to include many creatures neither huge nor monstrous—is as old as humanity itself.

In 1982, a group of scientists from North America and Europe formed the International Society of Cryptozoology (ISC), with Dr. Heuvelmans as president, to place their research on an organized and scientific basis. Financial problems forced the ISC to disband after 1996, but its work is carried on today by Canada's British Columbia Scientific Cryptozoology Club and England's Centre for Fortean Zoology.[3]

Dr. Heuvelmans defined cryptids as "unknown animal forms about which only testimonial or circumstantial evidence is available, or material evidence considered insufficient by some." ISC members, at their first meeting, broadened that definition to include "the possible evidence of *known* animals in areas where they are not supposed to occur (either now or in the past) as well as the unknown persistence of presumed extinct animals to the present time or to the recent past... What makes an animal of interest to cryptozoology...is that it is *unexpected.*"[4]

Author Chad Arment published the first (and only) textbook on cryptozoology in 2004, listing four broad categories of cryptids.[5] They include:

1. Animals similar to known living species but with obvious physical differences, such as spotted lions, pygmy elephants, or 80-foot anacondas.

2. Animals similar to known living species but found far outside their normal geographical range, such as kangaroos or "black panthers" in Britain.

Persistent reports describe living dinosaurs in Africa.
Courtesy of William Rebsamen

3. Animals resembling known extinct species, such as dinosaurs reported from the jungles of Africa and South America.

4. Animals apparently unrelated to any known species, either living or extinct, such as West Virginia's infamous "Mothman."

Many reports of cryptids come to us from distant foreign lands. Famous examples include Scotland's Loch Ness Monster, the Yeti, or Abominable Snowman of the Himalayas, the huge serpent known as Nāga in Southeast Asia, and the Mongolian "death worm." However, no passport is required to seek some of the strangest creatures said to live on Earth.

In every state across America, unidentified beasts are reported with surprising frequency. No state is free of such encounters, although some boast more than others. It may come as no surprise that California—which, through Hollywood, has brought us *Frankenstein* and *Dracula, The Mummy* and *The Wolf Man, The Creature from the Black Lagoon* and all manner of giant man-eating insects—has more than its share of monsters in the flesh.

Strange California Monsters is the first book to collect, review and analyze reports of monsters in all shapes and sizes from the Golden State. Previous works either focus exclusively on individual creatures, such as Randall Reinstedt's *Mysterious Sea Monsters of California's Central Coast* (1993), or combine unknown animals together with UFOs, hauntings, and other strange phenomena, as in Preston Dennett's *Supernatural California* (2006) and Joe Osterle's *Weird California* (2006).

This book includes eight chapters, topically arranged.

Chapter 1 examines California as a monster habitat, considering the likelihood that unknown creatures may exist in a state with more than 36 million human inhabitants.

Chapter 2 reviews sightings of monsters from the sea, from lakes and rivers, which defy classification.

Chapter 3 surveys reports of cryptic reptiles and amphibians, either unknown to science or discovered far outside their normal range.

Chapter 4 collects reports of monstrous birds and other unidentified flying creatures.

Chapter 5 tracks alien big cats throughout the Golden State.

Chapter 6 details California's history of Bigfoot/Sasquatch sightings, while ...

Chapter 7 dissects the controversy surrounding history's most famous film of a supposed unknown primate.

Chapter 8 completes the crypto-tour with reports of creatures that fit none of the previous categories.

Our quest may offer some surprises, possibly a shock or two, but never fear. The creatures you encounter in these pages cannot harm you.

As for those outside your window, lurking in the darkness...who can say?

Chapter 1

Unknown California

California is the Golden State, the Land of Opportunity—for millions, the literal end of the rainbow. Fame-seekers and fugitives in the United States can run no farther west without tumbling into the sea.

Geographically, California is the third-largest American state, sprawling over 163,696 square miles, but none other boasts a larger population. At last count, California harbored 36,457,549 people—12 percent of America's total population—for an average density of 224 persons per square mile. More than 19 million cars roll over California's 167,981 miles of recognized highways day and night, year-round.[1]

So California must be terminally crowded, right? That many people, jostling with tourists by the millions, must fill every corner of the state to overflowing.

Well, not quite. In fact, as we shall see, the Golden State has room to spare for mysteries of every kind, and ample space for unknown creatures to conceal themselves.

Who Lives Where?

First, we must recognize that 69 percent of California's human residents—more than 25 million people—live jammed together like ants in four urban centers comprising 5.6 percent of the state's total area. When we adjust state population figures to delete residents of Los Angeles, Sacramento, San Diego, and the San Francisco Bay Area, population density drops 67 percent, to 73 persons per square mile. Nine other cities—Bakersfield, Carlsbad, Concord, Fresno, Modesto, Oxnard, Riverside, San Bernardino and Santa Barbara—claim an additional 2.5 million residents. Statewide, the vast majority of Californians live within the boundaries of 478 incorporated cities and towns.[2]

Elsewhere, much of the state is wild, tainted by humans but untamed. California's diverse geography ranges from sandy beaches and rocky cliffs on the Pacific coast to looming mountains capped with snow, from trackless forests to arid, inhospitable deserts. Everywhere we turn there are natural wonders...and places to hide.

California boasts 42 mountain ranges, including the rugged Cascades (stretching for 700 miles, across the border into Oregon) and the majestic Sierra Nevadas (400 miles long). Mount Whitney, in the Sierras, is the highest peak in the contiguous 48 states, at 14,491 feet. Statewide, at least 99 other peaks exceed 13,000 feet.[3]

Most of those mountains bristle with trees. Overall, California has 18 national forests and 8 state forests, covering 31,927 square miles—19.5 percent of the state's total area. In the southeastern quarter, forest gives way to brutal desert. The Colorado Desert covers 2,500 square miles, while the Mojave (shared with Arizona and Nevada) and the Sonora (extending into Mexico) spread over 22,000 and 120,000 square miles, respectively.[4]

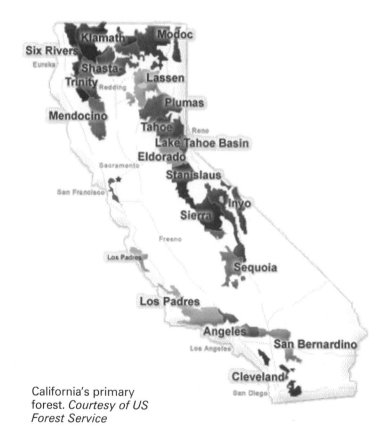

California's primary forest. *Courtesy of US Forest Service*

In and around those forests and deserts, California has 140 designated wilderness areas. The largest, in order of size, include:

Yosemite National Park: 1,189 square miles
John Muir Wilderness: 581,000 acres
Trinity Alps Wilderness: 525,627 acres
Ventana Wilderness: 240,024 acres
Ansel Adams Wilderness: 230,258 acres
San Rafael Wilderness: 197,380 acres
Old Women Mountains Wilderness: 183,538 acres
Emigrant Wilderness: 112,277 acres
San Gorgonio Wilderness: 94,664 acres
Owens Peak Wilderness: 74,640 acres
South Warner Wilderness: 70,385 acres
Dick Smith Wilderness: 67,700 acres
Desolation Wilderness: 63,690 acres
Hoover Wilderness: 48,601 acres
Ishi Wilderness: 41,000 acres[5]

All right, the skeptics say—but so what? Is it not true that every inch of California, whether inhabited or not, has been explored, surveyed, and mapped?

Well, yes...and *no*.

Maps of the Golden State exist, of course. They are remarkably detailed, including every city, town and village, each highway and railroad, most of the lakes, rivers, and mountain peaks. And yet....

When zoologist Ivan Sanderson prepared his classic global survey of unknown primates, published in 1961, he discovered that the region between San Francisco and the Oregon border had been "surveyed" only once—in *1859*. As Sanderson explained, "[T] he survey was ostensibly made on a 1-mile grid; that is to say the surveyor was supposed to walk a mile north, south, east, or west, take a fix and drive a stake, and continue doing this until he reached some previously selected line at the other end that linked up with the next survey."[6]

In fact, however, the land is so rugged that surveyors barely penetrated its fringes, marking locations of visible peaks and accessible settlements, following rivers or trails, and then completing grids on paper from a combination of logic and imagination. Page after page of the surveyors' notebooks—preserved to this day at San Francisco's Land Office—are totally blank. In later generations, aerial and satellite photography filled in some of the gaps, but those photos tell us little or nothing about the wildlife found at ground-level. In effect, much of that territory remains unexplored today.[7]

A case in point was reported by CNN News on August 12, 2005. The story concerned a 400-foot-tall waterfall located in the 43,000-acre Whiskeytown National Recreation Area, west of Redding, California. Although marked as "Whiskeytown Falls" on an ancient map, the waterfall stood forgotten, unknown to park officials and most local residents, until wildlife biologist Russ Weatherbee "discovered" it in August 2005.[8]

Whiskeytown Falls. *Courtesy of US Geological Survey*

And where a giant waterfall can be misplaced, what else awaits investigators?

Uninvited guests

California wildlife authorities recognize 132 species of freshwater fish, 51 amphibians, 84 reptiles, 634 birds, and 218 mammals (179 terrestrial and 39 marine) as full-time state inhabitants. Of those, "exotic" species introduced by humans since 1542 include 5 amphibians, 6 reptiles, 25 birds, 26 mammals, and 58 fish. The existence of 12 more fish species ranks as "uncertain," with a further 8 species listed as "hypothetical."[9]

Some of those alien drop-ins are startling. Among them, California's Department of Fish and Game numbers 10 species of parrots, parakeets, and macaws. Congress restricted importation of those birds in 1992, with passage of the Wild Bird Conservation Act, but the law backfired when various breeders released their birds to avoid prosecution. Today, parrots and related species have colonized the state from Kern County southward to the Mexican border. Flocks of 6,000 or more are reported from Los Angeles County.[10]

Some winged aliens arrive alone and stay that way. In November 2006, an East African crowned crane took up residence in an apricot orchard at Los Altos Hills, some 9,000 miles from its natural habitat. Seemingly unconscious of its honored role as Uganda's national bird, the crane was not a fugitive from any California zoo or the menagerie of any licensed breeder. Locals who sought advice on dealing with the bird were rebuffed by city police, sheriff's officers, and Wildlife Rescue. So it remains at large, sharing the food offered by neighbors with native quail and fending off cats who try their luck with the three-foot-tall bird.[11]

In California lakes and rivers, state authorities list the infamous South American piranha's status as "uncertain," and possession of piranhas is illegal, but the fish remain available for sale in other states and on the Internet. State wildlife officers acknowledge no piranha captures in California, but closely-related (and harmless) pacus have been hooked in California waters on at least two occasions. The first was caught in Fresno County, by a fisherman on the San Joaquin River,

Piranhas surface frequently in American lakes and rivers. *Courtesy of US Geological Survey*

15

in 1987. Another was pulled from a lake in Modesto, and promptly confiscated by game wardens, in July 2001.[12]

A more disturbing aquatic visitor, omitted from state lists of "uncertain" and "hypothetical" fish, is the snakehead. Science recognizes 33 species of snakeheads (Family *Channidae*) in two genera. All are native to Asia and Africa, voracious predators distinguished by long dorsal fins, large mouths bristling with razor-sharp teeth, and a physiological need to breathe atmospheric air through suprabranchial organs resembling primitive lungs. Their appearance and aggressive demeanor made snakeheads—dubbed "Frankenfish"—the subjects of four low-budget horror films produced in 2003-06.[13]

Channa argus (Cantor, 1842)
Northern Snakehead

After Berg, 1933

Snakehead fish threaten native wildlife in America. *Courtesy of US Geological Survey*

By that time, snakeheads had invaded the United States. The first known specimen was pulled from California's Silverwood Lake, in the San Bernardino National Forest, in 1997. Most journalists ignored that story, catching snakehead fever only after multiple specimens were caught in six East Coast states during 2001-04. Florida hosts the first established breeding colony of snakeheads, in Broward County, and while 13 states have thus far banned possession of Frankenfish, no officials claim that California is immune to infestation.[14]

Dead and Gone?

Spokesmen for the Fish and Game Department acknowledge only one species extirpated during California's long history—the sharp-tailed grouse—but others have been driven to the brink of extinction and displaced from their ancestral ranges by humanity's advance. North America's largest known bird, the California condor, once soared at will across the Southwest, but only 155 survive in the wild today, with another 147 in captivity. Presently, another 111 California species rank as threatened or endangered, including 26 fish, 21 mammals, 20 insects, 19 birds, 11 reptiles, 8 crustaceans, 5 amphibians, and 1 mollusc.[15]

California grizzly bears, though honored with a place on the state flag, were wiped out by hunters in 1922. Black bears have been more fortunate, but urban sprawl has still ejected them from areas they once inhabited—or, has it? In January 2005, the *San Francisco Chronicle* reported multiple bear sightings from the Bay Area's 1.2 million-acre greenbelt, including repeat appearances of a prowler known as the "Swanton Road Bear." Other ursine encounters occurred at Point Reyes, the Marin Headlands, and on the slopes of Mount Tamalpais.[16]

Ishi, the last of his tribe. *Courtesy of Michael Newton*

California's most startling "blast from the past" occurred on August 29, 1911, when residents of Oroville found a stranger huddled in a corral at a local stockyard. Butte County's sheriff took the man—an obvious Native American—into protective custody and subsequently delivered him to the Museum of Anthropology in San Francisco. There, Professors Alfred Kroeber and Thomas Waterman identified the man as a survivor of the Yahi tribe, a subgroup of the Yana people presumed extinct since the late nineteenth century.[17]

Kroeber and Waterman called their subject Ishi, the Yahi word for "man," since tribal custom forbade tribesmen from speaking their own names. Before tuberculosis claimed Ishi's life in 1916, the professors detailed his remarkable history. Born around 1860, Ishi lost most of his family at the Three Knolls Massacre of 1865, when ranchers murdered all but 30 members of the Yahi tribe. The rest went into hiding, hunted by whites who killed them on sight. All were presumed dead when Ishi surfaced in Oroville, the sole survivor of his people. Published estimates of California's total Yana population, prior to white invasion of the state, range from 1,500 to 3,000 individuals, occupying a territory of 2,400 square miles.[18]

Discoveries Galore

California's landscape and waters remain happy hunting grounds for zoologists in the twenty-first century. New species appear with surprising regularity in the sea offshore, in virgin woodlands—and even underground.

May 2003 brought the discovery of a new jellyfish from California's coastline, nicknamed "Big Red" by Dr. George Matsumoto at the Monterey Bay Aquarium Research Institute. The deepwater jelly's red body exceeds three feet in diameter, and it was deemed unusual enough to rate its own subfamily. Whereas most jellies are distinguished by a specific number of tentacles, Big Red (Latin name *Tiburonia granrojo*) has none, and the fleshy arms used to capture prey vary in number from one specimen to the next. "Diving almost every day," Dr. Matsumoto said, "we tend to take for granted some of the unusual and even bizarre animals that we see in the deep ocean. This just shows that we need to keep our eyes open, because there's still plenty to discover down there."[19]

Marine biologists got another surprise in July 2004, when California waters yielded two new species of blind bone-eating worms that feed on whale carcasses. Again, the creatures were unique, rating creation of the new genus *Osedax* ("bone-devouring"). Researchers found the first specimens feasting on a dead gray whale in Monterey Bay, at a depth of 9,100 feet. Only females were noted at first, until scientists found the microscopic males dwelling *inside* their finger-sized mates. DNA tests indicate that the worms evolved around 42 million years ago, at the same time as whales.[20]

Another surprise from the sea arrived in February 2005, with the discovery of a new coral species dwelling hundreds of feet below the Channel Islands, offshore from Santa Barbara and Los Angeles.

Dr. Milton Love, marine biologist at the University of California-Santa Barbara, identified the black coral and christened it *Antipathes dendrochristos*.[21]

Moving inland to the Siskiyou Mountains, we note the discovery of a new amphibian species in May 2005. The Scott Bar salamander apparently evolved during the Pleistocene epoch and survived the last ice age, from 1.8 million to 10,000 years ago. These salamanders have no lungs, but breathe directly through their skin. Joseph Vaile, spokesman for the Klamath-Siskiyou Wildlands Center, told reporters, "Everyone talks about how biologically rich the tropics are, but we are still discovering species right here in the Klamath-Siskiyou. This is really an exciting discovery."[22]

Eight months after that announcement aired, in January 2006, scientists reported discovery of 27 new animal species in caves beneath the Sierra Nevada Mountains. Joel DeSpain, who explored 30 of the 238 known caves in Kings Canyon and Sequoia National Parks, told reporters, "Not only are these animals new to science, but they're adapted to very specific environments—some of them, to a single room in one cave." Fellow explorer Jean Krejca, a biologist with Texas-based Zara Environmental, said of the new discoveries, "We don't know how long they live, what kind of habitat they prefer, how many offspring they have, or how sensitive they are to human disturbance. There's still so much to learn."[23]

As we shall see, the same is true of California at large, from its coastal waters to its lofty mountain peaks. We all have much to learn.

Let the adventure begin.

Chapter 2

From the Depths

Science tells us that all life began in the water, and so does our search for monsters. Throughout recorded history, seafarers have reported sightings of large unknown creatures, inscribing their charts with notations that read "Here Be Monsters." Today, some of those beasts are recognized as whales, whale sharks, and giant squids, but others defy identification. Likewise, sightings of freshwater "sea serpents" emanate from some 900 lakes and rivers worldwide.[1]

More than 70 percent of Earth's surface is covered by water, and California claims its share. The vast Pacific Ocean lies offshore, caressing 3,427 miles of tidal coastline including California's many bays and islands. The state also features 2,625 lakes and 98 significant swamps, fed by 9,893 rivers and streams—in short, water aplenty to nurture and hide all manner of aquatic or amphibious creatures.[2]

Many cryptozoologists apply the term dracontology to the specific study of large aquatic cryptids. Within that field, the focus may be further narrowed to encompass only marine animals (commonly called "sea serpents," although many are neither serpentine nor reptilian in form) or freshwater cryptids (often designated as "lake monsters," though some inhabit rivers). Bernard Heuvelmans proposed nine species of sea serpents in 1968, after reviewing 587 sightings logged between 1662 and 1966. Gary Mangiacopra narrowed the field to four species in 1977, based on his survey of 64 nineteenth-century cases, while authors Loren Coleman and Patrick Huyghe, writing in 2003, listed 14 cryptic marine species and four distinct freshwater species.[3] Mainstream science recognizes none of them, and we shall not concern ourselves unduly with attempts to classify the various unknowns.

Sea Serpents

While reports of large marine cryptids date from biblical times, and Native American mythology teems with aquatic monsters, California's published "sea serpent" sightings begin in the early twentieth century and continue through the twenty-first. The Golden State does not rival New England's whopping tally of reports, but large cryptids appear with sufficient frequency for authors Coleman and Huyghe to rank California's coast among Earth's "top eight places to look

for a sea serpent." In fact, they suggest that California's coastline "may be a playground and migration route for Sea Serpents, as it is for cetaceans."[4]

While that case remains unproven, there are sightings aplenty on record from San Clemente in the south, to San Francisco Bay in the north. We shall review them in their order of appearance, chronologically.

Mariners have reported sea serpents throughout history. *Courtesy of Michael Newton*

Newport Beach
(1901)

California's first reported sea monster was hooked at Newport Beach by a "Mexican Indian fisherman" on February 22, 1901. He displayed "four tentacles and a strip of flesh about six feet long" to prove his conquest, then led Horatio Forgy from Santa Anna to the tide pool where the creature lay dead. Forgy determined it to be an oarfish (Family *Regalecidae*) measuring "21 feet and some inches," weighing an estimated 500-600 pounds. Even so, it was no record specimen. Oarfish commonly exceed 20 feet, with the longest confirmed specimen stretching one inch beyond 36 feet. Some ichthyologists believe adult oarfish may top 50 feet, perhaps being responsible for many "sea serpent" sightings throughout history.[5]

Long Beach
(1909)

On February 19, 1909, five fishermen aboard the launch *Rita* met an unidentified creature at the Grouper Banks, 18 miles offshore from Long Beach, in Los Angeles County. Witness Guy Griffith told reporters, "The monster was about 40 feet long and about 15 feet back from the head it had a big dorsal fin. The head was as big as a barrel and brown with eyes as big as my fist and it moved from side to side. The tail was like that of a porpoise. We first sighted the thing 100 feet away. The head was then out of the water and I started to shoot at it, but feared it might become angry and wreck us, so I told one of the boys to start the engine and we glided away but the monster came after us. We gave the engine all she could stand and got away from the creature."[6]

Santa Barbara
(1909)

Our next report is sadly lacking in detail. On October 2, 1909, crewmen aboard the steamship *St. Croix* met a large unknown creature off the coast of Santa Barbara. In comments to the San Francisco *Examiner,* they described it as 60 feet long, with a head like an eel's, and a body as thick as a man's. Authors Paul LeBlond and

Edward Bousfield include the incident in their list of Cadborosaurus sightings, although that sea serpent normally frequents waters of the Pacific Northwest.[7]

Venice Beach
(1912)

Fishermen sometimes catch unknown denizens of the deep. One of the most peculiar on record was hooked at Venice Beach, near Los Angeles, in mid-November 1912. Newspaper reports described it as "five feet in length, black and green mottled, with a tail like that of a shark. It has a dorsal fin and four feet, shaped like those of a parrot. Its mouth resembles that of a Gila monster, while its head is a replica on a large scale of a California horned toad." The carcass was not preserved, and it remains unidentified.[8]

A Strange "Fish"
(1912)

Our next item appears to be unique in the literature of strange creatures hauled from the sea. It was reported by the now-defunct *Modesto News* in May 1912 and read as follows:

EIGHT-LEGGED FISH BARKS LIKE DOG
SAN DIEGO, May 22—An eight-legged fish, with a bark like a dog and a ravenous appetite, was caught in a net off the Lower California coast by Steve Ohio of the fishing launch *Panama*. The strange denizen of the deep, held captive in an improvised tank, was brought to San Diego and, with a rope around the neck[,] was led along the custom house wharf while a hundred curious persons looked on.
The strange, unclassified creature has teeth like a canine and gills and dorsal fins, as well as scales like a fish. It is two feet in length and slender. The feet are without nails and covered with a soft fur. It will not eat meat, but eagerly devoured raw potatoes whole and seemed fond of seaweed. It ate out of Ohio's hand, but could not remain out of water long.[9]

No further information is available concerning the strange creature or its fate.

The San Clemente Monster
(1914-54)

While some sea monsters surface once and then vanish forever, others lay claim to particular waters and show themselves repeatedly, for years or decades on end. A case in point is the San Clemente Monster, which haunted the Gulf of Santa Catalina and adjacent waters from the early months of World War I into the mid-1950s.

Various authors date early sightings of the still-unknown creature from 1914, but the first detailed account was filed in 1919 by Ralph Bandini, secretary of the local Tuna Club, and crewman Percy Neal. Their glimpse of the monster was brief, but Neal reported "eyes as big as plates."[10]

Ralph Bandini and companion Smith Warner got a better look at the beast in September 1920, while fishing for marlin a mile west of San Clemente Island's Mosquito Harbor. Bandini described the incident 12 years later, in his book *Tight Lines.*

> "All of a sudden I saw something dark and big heave up. I seized my glasses. What I saw brought me up straight!
>
> "A great columnar neck and head, I guess that is what it was, lifting a good 10 feet. It must have been five or six feet thick. Something that appeared to be a kind of mane of long coarse hair, almost like a fine seaweed, hung dankly. But the eyes—those are what held me! Huge, seemingly bulging, round—at least a foot in diameter!
>
> "We swung toward it....Then, even as I watched through the glasses, the Thing sank. There was no swirl, no fuss....Just a leisurely, majestic sinking—and it disappeared, about a quarter mile away."[11]

Bandini estimated that the beast was larger than the biggest living whale, although he only saw a portion of it raised above the waves. He saw the monster (or one of its relatives) twice more in later years, but never had as close a view again.[12]

George Farnsworth, one-time president of the Tuna Club, described his sighting of the creature in his *History of the Tuna Club,* privately published in 1948. Without providing a date, he wrote: "Its eyes were 12 inches in diameter, not set on the side like an ordinary fish, but more central. It had a big mane of hair about two feet long. We were within a hundred feet of it before it went down. This was no sea elephant. It was some kind of mammal, for it could not have been standing so long unless it was."[13]

Other Tuna Club witnesses included ex-presidents Jimmy Jump and George Thomas III, Joe Coxe, and J. Charles Davis II. All were widely respected as deep-sea fishermen, and all agreed with the descriptions of the beast provided by Bandini and Farnsworth. In fact, Davis observed, "It was almost as though a recording had been made and each man played the same record." He noted, however, that "these men were all interviewed separately AND NONE OF THEM KNEW THAT I HAD TALKED TO ANYONE ELSE ABOUT THE SAN CLEMENTE MONSTER!"[14]

The beast made itself scarce during World War II, but returned in December 1950 to be seen by postal worker Opal Lambert, as it swam 200 yards offshore from Summerland. Lambert watched the creature for 10 minutes, estimating that its head was raised 4 feet above the surface.[15]

The next sighting occurred on June 8, 1953, when the creature showed itself to fisherman Sam Randazzo and his 8-man crew in the Santa Barbara Channel. Randazzo told the Coast Guard, "We saw the Thing, estimated that it had a neck 10 feet long and between 5 and 6 feet thick. Its eyes were cone shaped, protruding, and about a foot in diameter."[16]

Fate magazine reported another sighting in October 1954, which Bernard Heuvelmans regarded with some suspicion. Barney Armstrong, captain of the *Sea-Fern,* allegedly saw the beast with passenger Orrel Reed Jr. Armstrong, described it as "sickly green," with a "head [that] was round, thorny, and seemed to have a kind of horn, like a cornucopia, hanging. Its mouth was two feet across." Armstrong saw only one eye, while Reed claimed to see two. Heuvelmans concluded that it may have been a wounded specimen. "If this was really the San Clemente monster," he wrote, "the afflictions on its head might almost explain its color."[17]

Witnesses Grant King and Phil Parker logged another atypical sighting in the latter weeks of 1954, while fishing from a boat off the coast of La Jolla. They came within 50 feet of the beast and watched it for 25 minutes, during which time Parker determined that "it had a head and shoulders like a bull gorilla and no face." Quite rightly, he decided, "It wasn't a whale and it wasn't a sea lion. And it sure didn't look like a snake."[18]

Or like anything else known to science.

Despite the last two incidents, Heuvelmans classified the San Clemente Monster as a "merhorse," one of nine hypothetical creatures which he proposed to explain the world's sea serpent sightings. Since the San Clemente beast has not appeared since 1954, the mystery remains unsolved.[19]

Moore's Beach Monster
(1925)

Confusion surrounds the first appearance of this sea serpent. Bernard Heuvelmans dates its arrival from 1927 but cites no specific cases, while George Eberhart places its premier outing in the early 1930s and a Santa Cruz-based website claims the first sighting occurred "shortly after World War II." Eberhart's first witness is an unnamed teenager who reported a beast with a 12-foot neck and a head resembling a giraffe's swimming beyond the breakwater of Monterey Bay on some uncertain date.[21]

We have a year, at least, for the next incident. Crewmen aboard the fishing boat *Dante Alighieri* were trawling the depths of Monterey Bay in 1938, when they met a black 30-foot beast with a fishlike tail and a huge white head. They described its face as resembling an old man's, with large eyes and a crescent-shaped mouth.[22]

"Old Man of Monterey Bay"
(1927-?)

In the midst of San Clemente's monster flap, a carcass washed ashore at Moore's Beach, in Santa Cruz, some 400 miles to the north. Charles Moore found the body in late May 1925 and snapped two photos, depicting a 35-foot creature with a head resembling that of a porpoise, a protruding ducklike beak, a serpentine body, and a short tail. After viewing the photos—which, in author George Eberhart's view, had suffered "some artistic tampering"—ichthyologist Barton Evermann visited the site and took the creature's skull to his lab at San Francisco's California Academy of Sciences. There, he determined that the "monster" was a specimen of Baird's beaked whale (*Berardius bairdii*), which may reach lengths of 42 feet.[20]

The following year, fishermen aboard the *Santa Anna*, seeking albacore nine miles south of the Point Piños lighthouse, passed within a few feet of what they believed to be a floating log. When they jabbed the "log" with a gaff, it sprouted fins and made off at top speed. The startled witnesses described it as seal-like, but "50 times" the size of a normal sea elephant (*Mirounga* sp.), which boasts a record length of 22.5 feet.[23]

After a two-year hiatus, the Old Man returned in June 1941, frightening fisherman Bill Totten so badly that he ran home screaming from the wharf and stayed away for several weeks. More sightings

The Moore's Beach carcass, 1925. *Courtesy of Michael Newton*

Monterey Bay. *Courtesy of US National Oceanic and Atmospheric Administration*

were logged after World War II, but their cutoff date is unclear. Bernard Heuvelmans dates the creature's last appearance from 1947, when it was mentioned in the April 12 issue of the *Saturday Evening Post,* but a September 1999 issue of *Metro Santa Cruz* put the last of fisherman Victor Ghio's multiple sightings "35 to 40 years" earlier, sometime during 1959-64.[24]

On December 19, 2008, television's Animal Planet channel premiered a new series entitled *Lost Tapes,* which claims to air videotapes recovered from the scenes of dramatic—even fatal—encounters between cryptids and human beings. The show's first segment, titled "Monterey Monster," related the supposed disappearance of journalist and yachtswoman Sharon Novak, lost at sea in Monterey Bay during December 2007. The half-hour episode consisted mainly of alleged footage from various cameras installed by Novak on her boat to chronicle her circumnavigation of the globe. In the final moments, after answering another boat's distress call and finding it abandoned, smeared with blood, Novak is pitched overboard and presumably devoured by a long-necked sea monster caught on tape as a shadow gliding beneath the water's surface.[25]

No scientific expertise is required to dismiss the tale as fictional. Aside from the improbable multitude of camera angles—including one atop the boat's mast, perfectly positioned to spy passing monsters, and another seemingly mounted on Novak's head as she falls overboard—Novak herself has proved untraceable. A search of the *Monterey County Herald* reveals no mention of a disappearing sailor during 2007, nor did *Lost Tapes* itself rate any morning-after mention for its startling report.[26]

San Francisco
(1935)

While anonymous Internet postings claim that sea serpent sightings in San Francisco Bay "go back over a hundred years," the first case noted in cryptozoological literature dates from 1935—and sadly, it says virtually nothing. Bernard Heuvelmans includes the incident in his 1968 listing of 587 alleged sea monster encounters, but he makes no mention of it in the body of his text. Worse yet, he lists no source and tags the year with a question mark, likewise the columns of his chart reserved for witnesses and tentative classification of the animal in question. Exhaustive searches failed to disclose any further details of the case, assuming it occurred at all.[28]

A Merman
(1935)

Crewmen aboard an unnamed fishing boat logged an atypical sea monster sighting from the waters off Redondo Beach, in May 1935. While trolling three miles offshore, they saw an apparent male merbeing, 10-12 feet long, with "shiny eyes under [a] broad, smooth forehead," framed by dark hair and a beard to match. The fishermen lowered a skiff to pursue the creature, whereupon it dived with a flick of its tail and did not reappear.[27]

Merbeings are not always
beautiful females.
Courtesy of Michael Newton

"Bobo"
(1936-46)

Opinions are divided over this strange beast, which showed itself to fishermen off Cape San Martin, 60 miles south of Monterey Bay, on November 7, 1946. George Eberhart considers it identical to the Old Man of Monterey Bay, yet includes a separate listing for the latter beast in his encyclopedia of unknown creatures. Bernard Heuvelmans, conversely, treats the two monsters as separate entities. He credits Bobo with "many witnesses," but names none.[29]

However many witnesses there were, they all agreed that Bobo was peculiar. Reporters for United Press International subsequently claimed that Bobo had been seen around Cape San Martin for 10 years, but no further sightings were detailed. The origin of Bobo's nickname is obscure, but Eberhart credits local Portuguese fisherman, noting that *bobo* translates from their native tongue as "silly."[30]

Carmel
(1948)

In April 1948, three men strolling along a beach near the mouth of Monterey County's Carmel River saw a large snakelike head rise from the water offshore. They later estimated that the creature's "pinkish" head and neck stood some eight feet above the surface, trailing a 40-foot body covered in greenish-gray hair, with a row of "green glassy spines" bristling along its back. The description fits no creature known to science.[31]

Redwood City
(1955)

Our next sighting provides more detail, including the name of a witness. Joseph Korhummel was hiking along the San Mateo County coastline near Redwood City, in July 1955, when he noticed something splashing in the sea offshore. Climbing atop some rocks to get a better look, Korhummel beheld a brownish-green creature of serpentine form, some 16-18 feet long and "at least a foot in diameter," sporting a fin close behind its head. Within moments, the beast swam away and disappeared.[32]

Venice Beach
(1955)

Five months after Korhummel's sighting, in December 1955, a strange carcass washed ashore at Venice Beach, in Los Angeles County, some 360 miles south of Redwood City. Overlooked by Dr. Heuvelmans and most other sea-serpent researchers, the serpentine body measured 16 feet long and 14 inches in diameter. Author John Keel notes that it "came complete with fins and a snakish head."[33]

Malibu
(1963)

The next California "globster," beached at Malibu on September 25, 1963, was more easily explained. It proved to be another oarfish, measuring 18 feet. Today, it may be seen by visitors to the Los Angeles County Museum of Natural History.[34]

A relatively small oarfish. *Courtesy of Michael Newton*

Stinson Beach Monster (1976-83)

Another 13 years elapsed before the next reported sighting of a sea monster in California waters, on September 30, 1976. Witness Tom D'Onofrio was a Methodist preacher-turned-artist, renowned as a master wood-carver, who glimpsed the creature while horseback riding with a friend on Agnate Beach, near Bolinas. Thirty years after the fact, he recalled his sighting for a local TV broadcast.

"It was a big glassy wave," D'Onofrio said, "and right in the wall of that wave was a dark object, big like 40, 50 feet long. And I looked at him and he looked at me and my eyes must of been like that, I mean it was like nothing I've ever seen. It was thick and it was wide and it had lots of body to it but it wasn't a whale—that's what I first thought, but it wasn't a whale because it was kind of doing like this. And it disappeared and I said what in the world is that?"[35]

Despite the passage of three decades, D'Onofrio still recalled the encounter as a "spiritual moment," carving a boat's figurehead in the monster's likeness.

"I was in the presence of something I couldn't cope with," he said, "so I went back, got on my horse, went back to the studio filled with this energy, this came to me to get this piece finished. I am going to loose this energy man, and I am going to finish this piece and I carved for four days. I never came out except to eat. It's affected everything I've done since then."[36]

Despite a brief mention of D'Onofrio's sighting in the *Great Western Pacific Coastal Report* for 1976, the Stinson Beach monster received no further media attention until November 1, 1983, when the beast showed itself to a six-member construction team working on Highway 1 above Stinson Beach. Flagman Matt Ratto saw the creature first, and grabbed a pair of binoculars. Crew spokesperson Marlene Martin later told author Michael Bright that the animal "must have been about 100 feet long, and like a big black hose about five feet in diameter. I didn't see the end of the tail." As the witnesses stared, it "made a U-turn and raced back like a torpedo, out to sea. All of a sudden it thrust its head out of the water, its mouth went towards the sky and it thrashed about. Then it stopped, coiled itself up into three humps of the body and started to whip about like an uncontrolled hosepipe. It did not swim sideways like a snake, but up and down."[37]

Artist's conception of Cadborosaurus. *Courtesy of William Rebsamen*

While the creature's mouth was open, Martin noted its even rows of "peg-like" teeth. She only saw one eye, but was impressed by its deep ruby red. "Never in my wildest dreams," she told Bright, "could I have imagined a thing to be so huge and go so fast." Steve Bjora, the crew's truck driver, estimated the monster's speed at 50 miles per hour. Authors Paul LeBlond and Edward Bousfield consider the Stinson Beach creature a specimen of their elusive Cadborosaurus.[38]

Costa Mesa
(1983)

On November 2, 1985, surfers reported a sea serpent sighting near Costa Mesa, in Orange County. They described the creature as resembling "a long black eel," and one witness told a local newspaper, "There were no dorsal fins. The skin texture wasn't the same as a whale, and when it broke water, it wasn't like a whale at all. I didn't see the head or the tail."[39]

From that sparse information, J. Richard Greenwell—secretary/treasurer of the International Society for Cryptozoology—concluded that the Costa Mesa creature was identical to the one seen off Stinson Beach two years earlier. Authors Colin and Janet Bord followed Greenwell's lead in 1989, mistakenly claiming that Costa Mesa adjoins Stinson Beach, when in fact the two sites are separated by some 370 miles. Author Richard Ellis takes a different view, suggesting that the surfers glimpsed one tentacle of a giant squid drifting near the ocean's surface.[40]

San Francisco Bay
(1985-2004)

On February 5, 1985, brothers Robert and William Clark parked their car on San Francisco's Marina Green near Stone Tower Point, to enjoy some coffee before going to work. Before them lay a panoramic view of San Francisco Bay, from Alcatraz Island to the Golden Gate Bridge. They were watching sea lions offshore, when "a long, black tubular object telescoped about ten feet straight up out of the water and then it lunged forward almost falling on top of the sea lions." The frightened mammals fled, but their unknown pursuer gave chase, revealing a "black and slimy" arch that "looked like half a truck tire." From a distance of 25 yards, the Clarks observed a 30-foot neck, ending in a head with prominent eyebrow ridges and a "short flat snout." When the beast rolled over, they beheld its cream-white underside with a hint of yellow, resembling an alligator's belly. Rather ominously, they observed that "[t]here was enough room to accommodate a human being inside it."[41]

Overall, the brothers estimated that the beast was 60 feet long. As it spun in the water, they glimpsed miniature "dragon's wings" on each side, further described as triangular "fan-like appendages" with serrated edges, composed of "paper-thin membrane" stretched over "mossy green ribbing." William noted two more appendages, one at each end of the creature's midline, resembling "stabilizer fins as opposed to flippers for propulsion."[42]

The beast soon vanished underwater, but the brothers returned on February 6 with a video camera. Nothing happened that day, but the Clarks saw their scaly visitor again on February 28 and March 1. Both sightings were brief and failed to produce any photographic evidence.[43]

Fog and pouring rain spoiled their next attempt to videotape the sea monster, on December 22, 1986, but the Clarks were still able to see its "flat snout with two black, oval nostrils as large as a man's fist" from a distance of 50-75 yards. William was alone the next morning, in another rain squall, when the beast reared its head five feet out of the water, then dived before Clark could focus his camera. Both brothers were present when the beast returned on January 24, 1987, and while they snapped a full roll of photographs, rain blurred the camera's lens and spoiled the shots.[44]

San Francisco Bay. *Courtesy of US Geological Survey*

On February 25, 1987, the Clarks logged a peculiar sighting of "two objects intertwined." One, they say, resembled a thin black hose, wrapped around a larger object "which was the arch of the creature." Fifteen minutes after it submerged, the serpent poked its head above water once more to emit sounds like a growl and hiss combined. William snapped several photos before it sank again, one of which purportedly reveals "a long, thin, black object" protruding from the water. Four days later, Robert saw "two arches moving in unison" along the surface, at a range of "several hundred yards."[45]

The Clarks grew tired of standing watch over the bay and focused on their paying jobs for the next 17 years, but they were present with a video camera when the monster surfaced again, on January 26, 2004. This time, the setting was Fisherman's Wharf, with a view of Alcatraz Island. They saw a veritable swarm of creatures—"dozens," by Robert's estimate—and William aimed his camera out to sea, filming for roughly four minutes before the battery died.[46]

The brothers now say that two scientific analyses have been performed on their videotape. Specifically: "One was done by BSM Associates (expert image analyst Clifford Paiva and physicist Dr. Harold Slusher) and the second was done by marine biologist Bruce Champagne. Both analyses concluded that our video contains images of several large unknown serpentine marine animals swimming in SF Bay." The report from BSM—a firm "actively involved in missile defense algorithm development guidelines for boost-phase intercept"—is unavailable, but research online identifies founder Clifford Paiva as a physicist and former image specialist for the U.S. Navy, whose interests range from rocket science to investigation of alleged remains of Noah's Ark. Critics have questioned Harold Slusher's academic credentials and note his involvement with the Institute for Creation Research, which maintains that Earth was created by God in six days, sometime between 6,000 and 10,000 years ago.[47]

No background information is available on Bruce Champagne, but his report is found online. After extensive discussion of tides, weather, and species normally encountered in San Francisco Bay, he concludes that the creatures shown on the videotape "do not appear consistent with the dimensions, behavior, capabilities, and/or characteristics of known species, phenomena, and design requirements, but do compare favorably by morphology and behavior to previously reported animals in the area, and that of the Type III Animal proposal. The video record suggests the possibility of large, formally undescribed marine animals in proximity to the eastern Pacific Ocean coasts and associated waterways." He then proceeds to classify them as "Type III Animals," which have been "recorded as early as 1746, and often regularly in predictable locations for extended periods of time."[48]

Freshwater Phantoms

Moving inland from the Pacific, we find nine California lakes and two rivers listed in cryptozoological literature as monster habitats. Three sites were known to aboriginal inhabitants as the domain of large, malevolent creatures, while others earned their reputations after European settlers arrived on the scene.

Homer Lake, in Lassen County (northeastern California, on the Nevada border), lies between Lassen Volcanic National Park and the Plumas National Forest. Members of the Northwest Maidu tribe believed it to contain a *manitou* (devil) that menaced humans who encroached upon its territory. No modern sightings are on file.[49]

Homer Lake. *Courtesy of US Geological Survey*

The Klamath River, California's third-longest, winds over 263 miles through northern California and southern Oregon. Native Americans dwelling along its course believed it was inhabited by creatures known as "water dogs." Meanwhile, Wintun tribesmen claimed that the Klamath's longest tributary—the 130-mile-long Trinity River—harbored fierce "water panthers." Again, no modern sightings have been logged from either river, although strange cryptid encounters are recorded from the surrounding Trinity Alps (see Chapter 3).[50]

Elizabeth Lake
(1780-1890)

Elizabeth Lake lies west of Palmdale, in Los Angeles County, surrounded by the Angeles National Forest. Spanish missionary Junipero Serra named it *La Laguna de Diablo*—"Devil's Lake"—in 1780, based on aboriginal reports that it contained a monster thought to be "the Devil's pet." That name lasted until the mid-1830s, when the lake was renamed "Rabbit Lake," then changed again to become *La Laguna de Chico Lopez*. Its modern name dates from 1849, when young Elizabeth Wingfield fell in and drowned, prompting locals to rename the lake in her honor.[51]

Renaming the lake did not get rid of its resident monster. Don Pedro Carillo blamed the Devil's pet for a fire that razed his ranch buildings in the early 1830s, while Anglo settlers in the 1850s reported strange cries in the night, accompanied by wicked visions that encouraged them to try their luck at farming elsewhere. Don Chico Lopez never saw the beast, but his livestock persistently vanished, while his employees reported a giant winged creature soaring over the spread by night. Lopez sold out in 1883 to his foreman, Chico Vasquez, who endured similar losses and finally departed.[52]

Elizabeth Lake. *Courtesy of US Geological Survey*

Descriptions of the monster varied from one encounter to the next, creating a composite creature with bat's wings, a bulldog's head surmounting the neck of a giraffe, a serpentine body 45-50 feet long, six legs or flippers, and stunning body odor. Don Felipe Rivera watched the thing eat one of his steers in 1886, while .44-caliber bullets bounced off its hide, and soon sold his ranch to Basque immigrant Miguel Leonis.[53]

Leonis ruled his empire like a warlord and brooked no interference from mere dragons. Legend has it that he confronted the monster in 1890, punching it in the eye when the beast again proved to be bulletproof. Folklorist Horace Bell claims that the monster then left Elizabeth Lake and flew off to Arizona, where the *Tombstone Epitaph* reported the slaying of "a winged monster resembling a huge alligator" on April 26, 1890.[54]

Proof of the Tombstone incident still eludes researchers, but the beast of Elizabeth Lake has not been sighted since 1890, although local newspapers still resurrect its legend on slow news days.[55]

Blue Lakes
(1870-71)

The Blue Lakes, consisting of Upper and Lower, cover 125 acres in western Lake County, northwest of Ukiah on Highway 20. Pomo tribesmen steered clear of the lakes, fearing contact with a monster that lived in their depths, but this time, encounters were also reported by white immigrants. In 1870, nine years after Lake County was formed from sections of Mendocino and Napa Counties, local farmers reported sightings of a 20-foot "dragon" paddling around the lakes. Reports continued into 1871, then ceased. The fate of the creature or creatures of Blue Lakes remains open to speculation.[56]

Pritchard's Lake
(1890)

Four months after the beast of Elizabeth Lake allegedly fell before cowboy guns in Arizona—on August 28, 1890—Yolo County's *Woodland Daily Democrat* reported "rather a fishy tale" from Pleasant Grove. Presumably, this was the Pleasant Grove community located then and now in nearby Sutter County, rather than the identically-named town later abandoned by its occupants in Tulare County,

216 miles farther south, but we cannot be sure. Confusion deepens with a reference to "Pritchard's Lake," a body of water found on no modern map of California.[57]

Borrowing its facts from the *Sacramento Daily Record-Union,* the *Daily Democrat* described a "great excitement" surrounding a reported "sea-serpent" in Pritchard's Lake. Unnamed witnesses described the beast as 30-40 feet long and seven feet in diameter at its thickest point, with "a great flat head and a pair of jaws that, when distended, could with ease admit a full-grown man. Those who saw it in the water describe it as being a very rapid swimmer, carrying its head at times about eight feet above the surface of the water."[58]

As the *Daily Democrat* went to press, the monster had not been seen for a week, but rancher J.R. Williams blamed it for devouring "a great many sheep." Professional hunter Pete St. Clair sought to earn a fortune by bagging the creature, dead or alive, but his quest proved fruitless. Some locals suggested that the monster had retired to Bartwell Lake—another site that proved untraceable during my research for this volume.[59]

Lake Elsinore (1884-1970)

With a surface area exceeding 3,000 acres, Lake Elsinore, in Riverside County, is California's largest freshwater body. Native Americans inhabited the area long before white settlers arrived, and the present-day town of Lake Elsinore was legally incorporated in 1888, five years before the creation of Riverside County. It was named for the Danish port city of Elsinore, setting for Shakespeare's *Hamlet,* which today is Lake Elsinore's "sister city."[60]

Lake Elsinore's resident monster—inevitably nicknamed "Elsie" and "Hamlet"—was a slow starter, logging its first appearance in 1884. Other sightings were reported in 1915 and 1933. On September 13, 1934, local rancher C.B. Greenstreet saw a beast 100 feet long, with a 30-foot tail. "I know you think I'm crazy," he told the *Los Angeles Times,* "but I saw it—we all saw it, my wife and two children—and my little girl was terrified." According to Greenstreet, the beast "would move along near the surface of the water lazy-like and then all at once would swish that huge tail and dart like lightning half the length of the lake."[61]

Lake Elsinore. *Courtesy of US Geological Survey*

It might seem difficult for Lake Elsinore to conceal a beast of that (or any other) size, since it looses 4.5 feet of water each year to dehydration, and it has been bone-dry at various times in the 1930s, in 1951 and 1955, and in the late 1960s. None of those droughts revealed a monster, nor was any washed into the surrounding landscape when the lake overflowed, flooding adjacent territory in 1980 and 1983.[62]

Nonetheless, sporadic sightings have continued from Lake Elsinore. During the drought of 1954, locals suggested that Elsie had found some other hiding place but would return when the lake was refilled. Sure enough, sightings resumed in 1967 and resident Bonnie Pray saw Elsie twice in winter 1970, describing it as 12 feet long and 3 feet wide, with a long head resembling a dinosaur's. Conversely, it swam by means of vertical undulations, a movement which no reptilian spine can achieve.[63]

Three park rangers subsequently saw Elsie/Hamlet, swimming within 50 yards of their boat, but the date of the sighting is unspecified. Author Loren Coleman claims "a series of good encounters" at Lake Elsinore in 1992, but provides no details. While there are no further sightings on record, Hamlet served as mascot for a minor league baseball team, the Lake Elsinore Storm, until 2002, and tourists may still visit the Elsie Museum in Lake Elsinore, at 199 West Graham Avenue.[64]

Lake Tahoe

Lake Tahoe sprawls for 191 square miles across the California-Nevada border, with two-thirds of its shoreline in Placer County, California, and the remainder in Washoe County, Nevada. It is 22 miles long and 12 miles across at its widest point. With a maximum recorded depth of 1,645 feet, it is America's second-deepest lake and the fifth-deepest on Earth, at 989 feet.[65]

Lake Tahoe. *Courtesy of US National Oceanic and Atmospheric Administration*

In short, there should be ample room to hide the monster (or *monsters*) that locals call "Tessie."

While various published accounts refer vaguely to Tessie sightings in the "mid-1800s," and folklorist Charles Skinner briefly mentioned the monster in 1903, no detailed sightings were recorded until the mid-1970s. According to modern legend, French oceanographer Jacques Cousteau led an expedition to Lake Tahoe sometime in the Seventies and emerged from its waters shaken, declaring, "The world isn't ready for what's down there!" Some Internet theorists suggest that "a stop was quickly put on [Cousteau's] mission by some powerful people"—perhaps wealthy gangsters who ran the nearby Cal-Neva Lodge through front man Frank Sinatra.[66]

In fact, while mafiosi certainly inhabited the region, Jacques Cousteau never set fin in Lake Tahoe. Son Philippe *did* visit the lake in April 2002, but nothing suggests that he met strange beasts in its depths.[67]

Meanwhile, Tessie sightings proliferated in the 1980s. Off-duty police officers Kris Beebe and Jerry Jones were water-skiing at Tahoe in June 1982, when they saw a "huge dark animal" surface within 25 feet of their boat. Two years later, on June 17, 1984, witnesses Patsy McKay and Diane Stavarakas saw a hump-backed creature 17 feet long surface repeatedly. In April 1985, Virgil Anderson and Mike Conway filmed a large unidentified animal cleaving the surface of Zephyr Cove, on the Nevada side.[68]

Witness Andrew Navarro reported another 1985 sighting to the British Columbia Scientific Cryptozoology Club in 1991. As he described it, Navarro was aboard a "party boat," passing King's Beach on the lake's northern shore (California side), when he and a companion saw "water shooting out of the lake, like when a whale blows water out of its blow hole." Next came the "hump of a brown creature" that swam in a circle for roughly three minutes, then submerged. "My first thought," Navarro told BCSCC president John Kirk, "was it was a whale, since the creature had to be huge from the size of the hump." Its movements were "more up and down, not side to side like a snake."[69]

Descriptions of Tessie vary dramatically, with estimates of its length ranging from 12 to 25 feet and larger. Local rumors claim that several unnamed fishermen have hooked the monster, only to have their lines snap—or to haul up bodies dumped by gangland hitmen, dressed in clothing from the days of Prohibition. Plans to explore the lake's depths with midget submarines thus far have not been carried out. The most recent Tessie sighting was logged by visitors Beth Douglas and Ron Talmage on April 22, 2005. They described a large creature with three to five humps on its back, breaking the surface 100 yards offshore from Tahoe Park Beach. "There were no big boats [on the water]," Talmage told reporter Keith Sheffield. "I thought[,] 'Whoa, this sucker's real.'"[70]

Like Elsie at Lake Elsinore, Tessie has its own museum for tourists, located at 8608 North Lake Boulevard in Kings Beach, California.[71]

"Hodgee"

Lake Hodges Reservoir lies on the San Dieguito River, 31 miles north of San Diego. It was created during World War I, when the San Dieguito Mutual Water Company spent $350,000 to build the Lake Hodges Dam, completed in January 1919. The Bernardo Station Bridge, spanning the reservoir, was also built, for an additional $80,000.[72]

Lake Hodges. *Courtesy of US National Oceanic and Atmospheric Administration*

Prior to construction of the dam, members of the aboriginal Kumeyaay tribe warned of a river monster inhabiting the San Dieguito, but modern rumors of the creature nicknamed "Hodgee" date from 1921, when two mining companies began extracting stone with heavy equipment. Local fishermen reported "a large disturbance" in Lake Hodges, prompting U.S. Navy spokesmen to deny that submarines were being tested in the reservoir. Fishermen filed more complaints in 1923, shortly before the rival mining firms found their gear crushed and toppled in nocturnal raids, staged four nights apart. San Diego County's sheriff reported that the unknown vandal(s) had traveled by water and "wiped away footprints."[73]

In 1929, Mayor John Offitt of suburban Escondido requested an investigation of monster reports from Lake Hodges. San Diego Mayor Harry Clark passed the job off to the Scripps Institution of Oceanography, founded in 1903 and housed since 1912 at the University of California-San Diego. Researchers found no conclusive proof of Hodgee's existence, but one team member saw an unknown creature's "lizard-like" head "protruding from the surface" of the reservoir. A Scripps internal memo, penned in 1930, recommended further investigation.[74]

The mystery deepened in 1931, when a boat docked at a small pier on Lake Hodges was demolished. Police found no tracks on the adjacent beach, concluding that the damage had been caused by "great turmoil under the water along the base of the pier, from a boat or underwater vessel...or perhaps a large creature." The following year, Scripps director Thomas Vaughan supervised construction of a large underwater trap, baited with a live sea lion pup and flanked by cameras submerged in glass boxes. Something took the bait and left behind a murky photo of what some viewers believe may be a long-necked beast resembling a *plesiosaur* from the Cretaceous Period. Subsequent attempts saw cameras and buoys smashed, before public outcry over use of sea lions as bait canceled the project.[75]

Nine years of inactivity ensued, before Scripps administrators joined the U.S. Navy's Office of Naval Research for a new approach. In 1941, fishing was banned from a large portion of Lake Hodges, while divers placed a trip-wire attached to a bank of cameras 12 inches below the lake's surface. Internet sources report three months of frustration, broken by the capture of "another incredible photo," but that shot has never been published. The Japanese raid on Pearl Harbor distracted naval leaders in December 1941, and research at Lake Hodges was suspended for the duration of World War II.[76]

In 1956, wildlife officials poisoned Lake Hodges with huge doses of rotenone, a broad-spectrum pesticide ostensibly deployed to extirpate invasive carp, which had the side effect of killing off most other aquatic life in the reservoir. Some observers speculated that the action was prompted by Hodgee, and that view was supported by an anonymous memo, written on City of San Diego stationery, stating that the government desired to eradicate all life forms in the lake, monstrous or otherwise.[77]

If true, the effort failed. Despite another lake-closing to fishermen in 1958, for "scientific studies," sightings of Hodgee continued. Sadly, few details were recorded, and no comprehensive list of sightings exists. San Diego journalist Christine Tapia writes that monster reports escalated "during a 19-year period that started in 1958," while San Dieguito River Park spokesmen claim the last sighting occurred in

1966. That event involved two picnicking families, seven witnesses in all, and produced a photo of some dark, humped object in the water, 50 yards offshore.[78]

In the 1970s, researchers from California State University and the California Division of Mines and Geology discovered an earthquake fault bisecting the bed of Lake Hodges. That announcement prompted speculation that Hodgee found its way into the reservoir from some subterranean vault, but other theorists suggest the creature may have entered via the San Dieguito River, which joins the Pacific Ocean at Del Mar. Mainstream scientists deny that any unknown creatures inhabit the lake, while members of the privately-funded Lake Hodges Scientific Research Center continue the search for Hodgee.[79]

Officials lifted the fishing ban at Lake Hodges in 1977, ending a 19-year hiatus. Eight years later, local angler Gene Dupras caught the second-largest U.S. bass on record, weighing 20 pounds 5 ounces. That same year, 1985, retiring damkeeper Morgan Tidwell added his name to the list of alleged Hodgee witnesses. In 2001, a San Diego reporter blamed Tidwell for promoting "a spoof initiated by a village newsletter."[80]

If Hodgee does exist, its habitat has suffered repeated pollution by ruptures of a sewage line laid across the reservoir's bottom. The line first broke in 1981, spilling 45,000 gallons of effluent. Two breaks in 1987 expelled 300 gallons and 3,000 gallons, respectively. Another break in 1990 poured 14,400 gallons of sewage into the lake. The worst leak of all—so far—occurred in 1998, when 1.5 million gallons of raw waste poisoned the reservoir.[81] All things considered, it's enough to keep Hodgee in a monstrous mood.

Lost Lake
(1971)

The rumored giant catfish of Lost Lake cannot match Hodgee's history, and its brief story is mired in unfortunate confusion. Loren Coleman reports that the sighting occurred in summer 1971 "at Lost River and Lost Lake just north of Fresno." Unfortunately, Fresno County has *three* Lost Lakes, all north of the city—and it has no Lost River. There *is* a Lost Creek, which apparently does not feed any of the three Lost Lakes. California's only Lost River flows through Modoc and Siskiyou Counties, on the Oregon border.[82]

Lost Lake. *Courtesy of US Geological Survey*

Coleman says that witness Cynthia Fairburn was lounging near the water with a friend when her companion cried out in surprise, drawing Fairburn's attention to a giant fish some 8-10 feet long. It was "headed for the lake downstream," and looked "shiny black, rather than scaly." The girls surmised that it was a huge catfish.[83]

Such monstrous catfish do exist, but not officially in the United States. The Mekong giant catfish (*Pangasianodon gigas*) lives in Southeast Asia, where a specimen caught in 2005 measured 8 feet 9 inches long and weighed 646 pounds. The wels catfish (*Silurus glanis*) of Eastern Europe holds a record of 8 feet 8 inches and 196 pounds. Meanwhile, the U.S. record catfish, caught in Texas during January 2004, measured five feet and weighed 121.5 pounds.[84]

Stafford Lake
(1984)

Stafford Lake, near Novato in Marin County, seems an improbable "monster" habitat. It did not exist until 1951, when construction workers completed the Novato Creek Dam and thus created a 195-acre reservoir used for drinking water, irrigation, and "improved navigation." Even so, reports of giant fish began to circulate among local residents—and they were proved true in August 1984, when the lake was drained to permit repairs on the dam. Dead in its dried-out basin, laborers found a white sturgeon (*Acipenser transmontanus*) measuring 6 feet 5 inches long and weighing 125 pounds. Ichthyologists at San Francisco's Steinhart Aquarium, where it was placed on display, estimated that the fish was over 50 years old. They offered no suggestion as to how it reached the reservoir.[85]

Stafford Lake. *Courtesy of US Geological Survey*

Clear Lake
(1993)

In October 1993, fisherman Lyle Dyslin reportedly caught a strange-looking fish at Clear Lake. It "resembled a coelacanth"—the famous fish presumed extinct for 65 million years, until one was caught alive off South Africa's coast in 1938—but it also somehow reminded Dyslin of his dachshund. Overcome by sympathy, he photographed the fish and then released it.[86]

Or so the story goes.

George Eberhart speculates that Dyslin actually caught a deformed catfish "or, less likely, a dramatic new species." Sadly, our search for further details is frustrated by the fact that California has no less than *nine* Clear Lakes, scattered over seven counties. Lake and Monroe Counties each have two lakes tagged with the popular name. At press time for this book, Clear Lake, Lyle Dyslin, and his fish remained untraceable.[87]

Clear Lake. *Courtesy of US Geological Survey*

Chapter 3

In Cold Blood

The first vertebrates to emerge from prehistoric seas were amphibians, broadly defined as creatures that spend at least part of their lives in water and do not produce via amniotic eggs. Most amphibians are not adapted to a full-time life on land. They breathe in varied ways, some using lungs, while others employ gills or breathe through their skin.[1]

Over eons, some amphibians evolved into reptiles, air-breathing species whose skin is protected by scales and which bear embryos surrounded by an amniotic membrane. While some reptiles maintain an amphibious lifestyle and a few spend their whole lives in water (except when emerging to lay eggs on land), most of the 8,225 species presently known to science are fully terrestrial.[2]

Both amphibians and reptiles are "cold-blooded" creatures, a misnomer commonly applied to ectotherms whose body temperature is determined by that of their environment. Such animals are also called poikilotherms ("of varying temperature"), as they lack the internal temperature-control mechanism enjoyed by birds and mammals. Their range of habitats is thus determined—at least in theory—by climate and seasonal temperatures that permit them to hunt and perform other functions without freezing.[3]

California's Department of Fish and Game (DFG) recognizes 67 amphibian species and 93 species of reptiles inhabiting the Golden State.[4] Our interest, however, lies with those not recognized and the surprises they may hold in store.

Giant Salamanders

Salamanders (Order *Caudata/Urodela*) include 560 species divided into nine families. The largest known species on Earth are the Chinese giant salamander (*Andrias davidianus*), with a record length of 5 feet 11 inches, and the Japanese giant salamander (*A. japonicus*), at 4 feet 9 inches. North America's largest known species is the hellbender (*Cryptobranchus alleganiensis*), officially confined to the eastern U.S. with a maximum length of 29 inches. California's largest known salamander, the Pacific giant (*Dicamptodon ensatus*) may reach 14 inches in rare cases, but normally does not exceed 6¾ inches.[5]

Nonetheless, reports of truly giant salamanders have emerged from northern California, spanning half a century, and have inspired repeated searches, all so far in vain.

A Pacific giant salamander. *Courtesy of US Fish & Wildlife Service*

Our first report of giant salamanders is unfortunately vague. Attorney Frank Griffith from Weaverville was hunting deer in Trinity County, sometime in the 1920s, when he allegedly saw five huge salamanders lying in the water of an unnamed mountain lake. He estimated that they ranged from five to nine feet long. Griffith reportedly hooked one but was not strong enough to pull it from the water. Afterward, he could not name the lake—Trinity County boasts 104—and in fact could not decide if the event occurred along New River or the North Fork of the Trinity.[6]

Griffith described his encounter to John Hubbard, an engineer at Keystone Mine (a Griffith legal client), and Hubbard repeated the tale to biologist Thomas Rodgers, at Chico State College, in 1948. Rodgers subsequently made four visits to the region, and while he found nothing, he speculated that Griffith might have seen freak specimens of *D. ensatus,* grown far beyond normal size due to isolation from others of their species.[7]

There the matter rested until June 1951, when herpetologist George Myers published an article in the scientific journal *Copeia,* describing his own encounter with a large amphibian in 1939. According to Myers, a commercial fisherman on the Sacramento River had found the animal trapped in one of his nets, and Myers had studied it for 30 minutes. It was, Myers wrote, "a fine *Megalobatrachus* [a genus of the family *Cryptobranchidae*] (unquestionably identified generically by its closed gill openings), in perfect condition."[8] He went on to say:

"It was between 25 and 30 inches in length....The creature exhibited coloration quite at variance not only with that of the several live Japanese examples I have seen, but also with the published accounts of the color of Chinese specimens. The dorsum was a uniform dark brown, with an irregular sparse sprinkling over all the back of rather well defined dull yellow spots, these being of irregular outline and about one centimeter in diameter. There were no small spots, darker than the ground-color, which is the common color patter of all the examples of *Megalobatrachus* I have seen, and the ground-color was definitely brownish, not slaty gray. Also, it must be emphasized that there was nothing to indicate that the coloration was due to disease. The animal appeared to be in the very best of condition.

"The source of the specimen is, of course, unknown. Its strange coloration even suggested the possibility of a native Californian *Megalobatrachus,* which would not be zoogeographically surprising, but no other captures have been reported."[9]

Another nine years passed before the giant salamanders re-surfaced. In January 1960, Vern Harden, an animal handler from Pioneer (in Amador County) allegedly caught a salamander 8 feet 4 inches long at a small lake in the Trinity Alps, then released it when a sudden snow storm threatened to trap him. Harden told his story to Victor Twitty, a biologist at Stanford University, who deemed the tale "spectacular, if true." Rev. Bernard Hubbard—brother of mine engineer John Hubbard, who apparently participated in two fruitless searches for giant salamanders during 1958-59—told the *Humboldt Times,* "Yes, I know Harden. He's a nice fellow who ought to write fiction."[10]

While Rev. Hubbard dismissed Harden's story, Texas oilman Tom Slick paid closer attention. By 1960, Slick had already financed two expeditions to locate the Yeti of the Himalayas and a search for Bigfoot in British Columbia. Now he focused briefly on the quest for giant salamanders, but like those who had preceded him, Slick went home empty-handed.[11]

On September 1, 1960, Thomas Rodgers joined Robert Stebbins from the University of California-Berkeley and Nathan Cohen from Modesto Junior College for another salamander hunt. They were accompanied by seven Explorer Scouts, scout leader Don Rodgers (Thomas's brother), and an unidentified man. Rodgers did not publish the results of that search until 1962, but the outcome was yet another disappointment. Giving up for good, he wrote, "It is hoped that this evidence will kill rumors about any giant salamanders (much less *Megalobatrachus*) in the Trinity Mountains of California."[12]

Of course, it did not kill the "rumors," and while no more sightings have been publicized since 1960, San Francisco author Kyle Mizokami put his Bigfoot research on hold to pursue a fruitless Trinity Alps Giant Salamanders Expedition in 1997. Loren Coleman and coauthor Patrick Huyghe, writing in 2003, referred to a giant salamander sighting at Fish Lake, but they provided no further details. Since California has *two* Fish Lakes, one each in Humboldt and Siskiyou Counties, that case has proved impossible to document.[13]

Crocodilians

Science recognizes 23 crocodilian species, including the alligators, caimans, crocodiles, and gharials. Two species—the American alligator (*Alligator mississippiensis*) and the American crocodile (*Crocodylus acutus*)—are native to North America, but neither naturally occurs in California or adjoining states.[14] That fact, however, has not prevented various crocodilians from appearing in the Golden State over the past eight decades.

The state's first alligator at large was reported in summer 1930 from Corcoran, in Kings County. Witnesses who saw it swimming in the Tulare Lake Canal described the beast as six feet long, but it was never caught.[15]

The next rogue gator turned up in Sacramento County's Folsom Lake, in September 1957, and appeared repeatedly to startled witnesses through June 1958. Loren Coleman suggests that several different reptiles were seen in the lake, but since none were captured, the question remains unanswered.[16]

Alligators are not native to California. *Courtesy of US Fish & Wildlife Service*

Late in 1960, the occupants of a Long Beach home (Los Angeles County) heard a heavy thump and a loud grunt from their backyard, emerging from the house to find a 5-foot crocodile lying on their lawn. In the absence of another explanation, they assumed the beast had fallen from the sky.[17]

Fifteen years later, in October 1975, another crocodilian visited Contra Costa County. Two patrolmen from the East Bay Regional Park District sighted the eight-foot reptile swimming in Lafayette Reservoir, on October 23. A search of the manmade lake followed, including boats, helicopters, and spotters on horseback, but the presumed alligator escaped and was not seen again.[18]

Loren Coleman reports that a four-foot crocodilian was seen at "Kings River, Fresno" on June 23, 1981. No further information is available.[19]

The next recorded gator sighting in the Golden State dates from summer 1996, when a reptile dubbed "Golden Gator" appeared in Mountain Lake, near San Francisco's Presidio. Sightings began on August 12 and precipitated a 10-week media circus, ending when San Francisco Zoo employees John Aikin and Woody Peterson caught the three-foot alligator in early October. As usual, the animal's presumed owner was not identified.[20]

While Golden Gator dodged hunters and journalists in 1996, a dead caiman was found at Lake Chabot, a reservoir in nearby Alameda County. Six years later, in July 2002, fisherman Jim Percival claimed repeated sightings of another caiman at Lake Chabot. His latest encounter had occurred "a few months" before the July 5 report, said Percival, but local wildlife officials ridiculed the claim, noting that one of Percival's corroborating witnesses was dead, while another was blind. Curiously, Lake Chabot has also produced tales of a "giant sturgeon" and a "five-foot catfish," both of which remain as elusive as Percival's caiman.[21]

San Diego policeman Ken Verdone was off duty, enjoying some time with his daughter at Chula Vista's Heritage Park on December 21, 2005, when he spotted a three-foot alligator paddling in a pond. Verdone summoned a park employee, who in turn called reptile wranglers from the San Diego Zoo to bag the scaly interloper. No one knows where the gator came from, but county spokesperson Diane Howell stated the obvious: "He wasn't there when we built the pond."[22]

California's most famous gator-at-large was "Reggie," who surfaced at 53-acre Machado Lake, in Harbor City's Ken Malloy Harbor Regional Park (Los Angeles County), in August 2005. Sightings began on August 10, followed two days later by confirmation from Harbor Regional Park ranger Lev Shaibi that the reptile was "a pretty decent size. He's going to be something to reckon with." That proved to be an understatement, and officials closed the lake to public access when initial bids to catch the reptile failed. Trappers from Exotic Wildlife, a Colorado firm "specializing in caimans," likewise failed to bag Reggie, while local councilwoman Janice

Hahn noted prior crocodilian reports from Machado Lake. "There have been alligator sightings out there, so we're not really sure how long he's been in there," Hahn told reporters. "For a long time, I think people thought it was an urban legend."[23]

Subsequent efforts proved no more effective, as Reggie evaded one team of searchers after another. Crowds turned out to watch the show, while "expert" trappers came and went, empty-handed. Officials declared a moratorium on gator-hunts, and police jailed two men suspected of releasing Reggie at Machado Lake. Officers seized other reptiles in that raid, including several alligators, but they failed to prove their case at trial. Firefighters caught a "skinny" three-foot gator—inevitably dubbed "Little Reggie"—in a flood-control channel near Machado Lake on September 8, but a September 13 Associated Press report of Reggie's capture proved to be a hoax.[24]

In fact, Reggie was still at large in June 2006, prompting Janice Hahn to complain, "All these important things I've done in my political career, every one, it doesn't matter. Distinguished doctors...at the grocery store, I'm getting my hair done, I was at my son's graduation at Pepperdine [University] a couple of Saturdays ago—people were coming up to me and asking, 'How's Reggie?' Running the second largest city in the country, all I'm going to be known for is, 'Where's Reggie?'" Nor had that question been answered by April 2007, when new sightings of a seven-foot gator emerged from Machado Lake. On that occasion, Hahn declared, "Reggie is older, Reggie is bigger and he's probably hungry, so I want to make sure that we keep the public safe. A live alligator in a public lake might be very hungry. It makes me a little nervous." The end came at last when Reggie was captured on May 24, 2007, and transported to the Los Angeles Zoo.[25]

"Old Bob"

California's Department of Fish and Game recognizes 12 native turtle species inhabiting the state. Excluding sea turtles, the largest acknowledged species is the snapping turtle (*Chelydra serpentina*), which may boast a shell 18.5 inches long. Snappers are an eastern species, but have been imported and established in the wild around Santa Barbara, with isolated specimens found elsewhere in the Golden State.[26]

In the early 1960s, residents of Fullerton, in Orange County, began reporting glimpses of a much larger turtle in Laguna Lake. Witnesses estimated that the elusive reptile weighed 100 pounds or more, triple the average weight of a common snapper. Locals dubbed the turtle "Old Bob," debating its existence over four decades until the mystery was solved at last.[27]

In September 2004, Laguna Lake was scheduled for a $2 million restoration project, which necessitated removal of fish and other aquatic wildlife. On September 10, while netting catfish, bluegills and other denizens of the reservoir, contractors unexpectedly snared Old Bob. He proved to be an alligator snapper (*Macrochelys temminckii*) with a 36-inch shell.[28]

The alligator snapper is America's largest turtle. *Courtesy of US Fish & Wildlife Service*

Like their smaller relatives, alligator snappers normally inhabit the eastern United States, ranging from Florida to Texas and northward into parts of the Midwest. Possession of alligator snappers is banned by law in California, and Old Bob's presence in Fullerton remains unexplained. Herpetologists estimated his age at 50 years, approximately half the normal life span for his species. Sharon Paquette, vice president of Orange County's chapter of the California Turtle and Tortoise Club, petitioned to keep Old Bob as an educational exhibit for children, but her request was denied and authorities moved the turtle to one of California's 350 wildlife preserves.[29]

Leaping Lizards

Lizards are reptiles of the order *Squamata,* normally possessing four legs and external ears. State wildlife authorities list 42 species as known inhabitants of California. The largest is the Gila monster (*Heloderma suspectum*), a venomous desert-dweller that may reach two feet in length. Old World monitor lizards (family *Varanidae*) grow much larger—including the Komodo dragon (*Varanus komodoensis*), which may reach 10 feet and ranks as Earth's largest lizard. While alien to North America, many monitors have reached the continent through traffic in exotic pets. Nile monitors (*V. niloticus*) now breed at large in southern Florida, where they reach lengths of 6-7 feet.[30]

The Komodo dragon, world's largest lizard. *Courtesy of US National Oceanic and Atmospheric Administration*

The exotic lizard trade does not explain an incident reported from Yolo County on August 8, 1891, by the *Woodland Daily Democrat.* According to that article:

> A young man of Woodland, noted for his veracity and temperance, has a strange story to tell. Last Tuesday night [August 4], together with some companions, he went to the Sacramento River

to fish. As they did not wish to begin until the early morning, they went to sleep beneath the blankets that they had brought with them. The young man...arose during the night to inspect some trout lines that he had set the evening previous. As he neared the bank, he could see that the water in the river was violently disturbed. He was much surprised at this, as he could see no boats either up or down the stream.

As he stood looking at the water, he saw, so he says, a head of what appeared to be a gigantic lizard stick up out of the water. He ran back to camp, and seizing a gun, retraced his steps to find the animal attempting to crawl upon the dry land. Raising his gun, he fired a shot at it, which evidently took effect, as the creature threw itself backward into the water with a loud splash, and commenced to swim down stream at a rapid rate, nearly a mile a minute, he thinks. The report aroused his friends, who rushed to the spot, only to catch a fleeting glance of the rapidly retreating monster.[31]

We should recall that the Sacramento River later produced a report of an alleged giant salamander (see above), although that specimen rivaled neither the size nor the agility of the monster seen in 1891.

Modern reports of monitors at large in California may indeed result from the escape or release of exotic pets. A four-foot-long Gould's monitor (*V. gouldii*), native to Australia, was captured at the Corda Dairy Farm, near the Marin-Sonoma County line, in July 2003. Alan Wold of Reptile Rescue made the catch, afterward telling reporters, "I've had monitor calls from Marin to Sonoma. Often, you get them in the neighborhoods." February 2006 brought reports of another four-foot monitor seen around Lake Otay, in San Diego, but that one—dubbed "Double X Lizzy" by locals—evaded pursuers and presumably remains at large today.[32]

The question, finally, is not whether monitor lizards exist in California: clearly, they do. Instead, we need to ask if anything prevents them from thriving and reproducing in the state's warm climate, as their relatives have done in Florida. The answer to that question seems to be a simple and resounding "No."

Snakes in the Grass

Of all reptiles, snakes elicit the most dramatic—and often negative—reaction from humans. California game wardens recognize 39 native species of snakes in their state, with the largest—the gopher snake (*Pituophis melanoleucus*)—claiming a record length of 8 feet 6 inches.[33] We are not shocked, though, to discover that reports of giant snakes have emanated from the Golden State since the mid-nineteenth century.

The gopher snake is California's largest native serpent. *Courtesy of US Fish & Wildlife Service*

The first sighting occurred at Spring Valley (Calaveras County) on August 12, 1868, but was not made public for over a decade. According to the Calaveras *Chronicle,* several witnesses saw the snake from "a considerable distance—never closer than a quarter of a mile," describing it as 40-60 feet long and "as big around as a barrel." The snake then disappeared for several months, before returning to frighten a miner named W.P. Peek, whose description included a most unsnakelike "screeching" sound. A year after that, the serpent terrified two boys at Mosquito Gulch, then vanished once more until August 24, 1878, when two hunters saw it from a range of 20 feet.[34] One witness, a Frenchman named Raud, described the beast as follows:

The serpent lay in three immense coils, the triple thickness of its body standing as high as my shoulders. The monster was fully 20 inches in diameter at the largest place. Its head was comparatively large. Its tremendous jaws at times dilated to twice their natural size, having enormous hooked fangs that fitted in between each other when the mouth was shut. The neck was slender and tapering. The belly of the serpent was a dirty whitish color, deeply furrowed with transverse corrugations. With the exception of about 10 feet of the neck and contiguous parts which were nearly black, the body of the snake was brown, beautifully mottled with orange-colored spots on its back.[35]

The snake eventually crawled away, permitting witness F.C. Buylick to judge its length "very exactly" from two nearby trees. The trees stood 40 feet apart, Buylick noting that the reptile's head was "even with one while its tail reached the other."[36]

While the giant Calaveras County snake was playing hide-and-seek with local residents, another large serpent appeared near Tres Pinos, in San Benito County. According to the Placerville *Mountain Democrat* of November 10, 1877, an unnamed local hunter shot a fawn and left it on the ground while he pursued other game, then returned to find a "huge serpent" coiled around the carcass. After shooting the reptile, the hunter paced off its length and declared it was 20 feet long, while its body was "as large around as a child's waist." The mighty hunter turned and fled moments later, when he saw more than 100 smaller snakes emerging from a nearby nest.[37]

The *Mountain Democrat* explained the incident by noting that a "serpent of the boa family" inhabits California. In fact, there are two—the rubber boa (*Charina bottae*) and the rosy boa (*Lichanura trivirgata*), each with one subspecies—but neither officially reaches four feet in length. The Tres Pinos monster remains unidentified.[38]

Daniel Cleve and T.O. Carter met an even larger snake while horseback riding through the Diablo Hills of Contra Costa County, in May 1878. The greenish-colored reptile was in "a semi-dormant state" when Carter killed it with a shotgun, measuring its carcass at 31 feet long and 3-4 inches in diameter.[39]

A rash of giant-snake reports emerged from the vicinity of Smartville (Yuba County) during 1880 and continued sporadically into summer 1884. Teamster Fred Campbell was the first named witness, claiming an encounter with a serpent "certainly over 51 feet" in length, whose body was "as large as a flour barrel." Other sightings were logged in the same period from French Corral (Nevada County) and Freemans Crossing (Sierra County). One Dr. Holdsworth, "an excellent and truthful" gentleman from Milton (Sierra County), saw a 20-foot snake "sporting" in a creek outside town, in June 1884.[40]

September 1882 brought reports of a "mammoth snake" prowling around the Sisquoc Ranch, 15 miles east of Santa Maria in Santa Barbara County. No eyewitness sightings were recorded, but locals described long drag-marks in the dirt that measured five inches across. They speculated that a recent drought affecting mountain streams drove the reptile to seek prey and water at lower elevations.[41]

Sightings resumed from Nevada County during 1895, when rancher George Wilmot of Grass Valley told the New York *Sun* that "there is a race, or at least a family, of monster snakes indigenous to the foothills of the mountains that rise above the Yuba River valley. That report recycled the Campbell and Holdridge sightings from 1880-84, while providing no new information.[42]

In January 1901, an unnamed Native American witness met a 25-foot snake "with huge jaws and flaming eyes" while hunting rabbits on property owned by William Ford, north of Ukiah in Mendocino County. According to the *Mendocino Democratic Daily,* the witness "was suddenly startled by a crackling sound in the bush, and glancing hastily behind him; he saw the dreaded monster coming swiftly toward him with head aloft and fury in his eye. The Indian immediately dropped his gun and fled, but the monster pursued him. He had two jack rabbits which he had killed and he threw these, one at a time to the serpent. In this way he gained a little on the serpent. For three miles the race continued and the Indian reached his camp in a state of collapse." Searchers failed to locate the creature, but the newspaper claimed that "for many years reports have been whispered about, especially among the Indians of this section, that an immense monster in the form of a serpent inhabits the hills north of Ukiah. The Indians have a tradition that many years ago this monster killed one of their strongest men. Since that time, the Thing has been occasionally seen always filling the hearts of those who see it with extreme terror and causing their instant flight."[43]

Ten years later, on August 31, 1906, Mrs. William Powell, her two children, and an unnamed female companion described a "boa constrictor" at large near Santa Rosa, in Sonoma County. The four were riding in a buggy outside town when they saw a supposed "huge log" lying beside the road. On closer inspection, it proved to be a 20-foot snake, more than two feet in diameter, with "a head as large as that of an ordinary child of 12 years." Newspapers claimed that the snake had "frequently been seen" around the Alexander Valley, "and more frequently signs of its existence have been found." One local, Joseph Alexander, claimed sightings of the snake spanning three decades, but the hunt he organized in September 1906 failed to bag the creature.[44]

An exotic visitor, the boa constrictor. *Courtesy of US National Oceanic and Atmospheric Administration*

In March 1911, residents of the Pinoleville Indian Reservation, near Ukiah (Mendocino County), complained of a giant snake circling their huts and hissing loudly after nightfall. The reptile was relatively small—about 10 feet long and as thick as "an ordinary stovepipe"—but newspaper reports claimed that "the reds" were too frightened to kill it. White hunters who answered the call for help found nothing, but a report in the Sheboygan (WI) *Daily Press* of March 23 referred vaguely to sightings in northern Sonoma and southern Mendocino Counties "for several years."[45]

Another 10-foot snake, this one said to be a boa constrictor with "baleful" eyes, frightened residents of Hayward (Alameda County) in June 1926. This time the reptile came with a back-story, rumors claiming that a four-foot "baby" serpent had escaped from a traveling circus several years earlier. The Oakland *Tribune* reported that sightings normally occurred on Saturday nights or Sunday mornings, perhaps implying that the witnesses were drunk, but gardener Juan Costa seemed sober enough. He saw the snake at 9 a.m. on June 10, then gathered a posse armed with "lassos, shotguns and monkey-wrenches," but failed to bag the reptile.[46]

A much larger snake, nicknamed "the sea-serpent of Old River," frightened residents of Contra Costa County during 1934. Witnesses—including the wife of an Antioch city councilman—saw the serpent "disporting itself" in swamps along the San Joaquin River. Finally, officials paid two unnamed hunters $50 to trap or kill the snake, which they supposedly accomplished by tear-gassing an abandoned mine on Mount Diablo, in the predawn hours of November 14. According to Reno's *Nevada State Journal,* the unidentified snake measured 25 feet long and 6-8 inches in diameter. Despite reported efforts "to locate the corpus delicti at zoos and other places in the Oakland and San Francisco districts," no trace of the captured snake could be found.[47]

We next leap forward to August 14, 1999, when witness Paul Roberts saw a snake 20-30 feet long, in or near the Sacramento River. Roberts reported his sighting to *Fortean Times* magazine, but details are sparse. Likewise, vague reports of a 20-foot python captured at Lake Chabot Regional Park, sometime before July 2002, include no substantive information.[48]

Skeptics presume that recent sightings or captures, at least, result from the escape or negligent release of exotic pets. They may be correct, since pythons are offered for sale through pet shops and Internet websites across North America. In Florida, Burmese pythons have colonized the Everglades, with 245 specimens captured by wildlife authorities during 2005-06 alone.[49]

Why should giant snakes, lizards, or crocodilians find California any less hospitable than Florida?

Chapter 4

Strange Skies

California wildlife authorities acknowledge 635 bird species as full- or part-time residents of the Golden State. Six other species are recognized as occasional visitors, without established breeding populations.[1] The state's largest known birds, in descending order of size, include:

- The California condor (Gymnogyps californianus), North America's largest living bird and the world's second largest, after the Andean condor (Vultur gryphus), with an average wingspan of 9 feet and a record of 11 feet 4 inches. The albatross (genus Diomedea) has a greater average wingspan than either condor, exceeding 11 feet, but they are smaller birds overall, with a record weight of 22 pounds versus the California condor's record of 31 pounds. Condors are vultures, with bare heads and necks, feeding primarily on carrion.[2]

- The golden eagle (Aquila chrysaetos canadensis), with a record wingspan of 7 feet 11 inches, and a top recorded weight of 15.4 pounds.[3]

- The bald eagle (Haliaeetus leucocephalus), boasting a record wingspan of 7 feet 4 inches and a maximum weight of 14 pounds. "Bald" eagles are not bald, in fact, as vultures are, but rather take their name from white plumage found on the head and neck of adult specimens.[4]

- The turkey vulture (Cathartes aura), a relative of the condors found throughout most of the Western Hemisphere, claiming a record wingspan of six feet and an average weight of 3.1 pounds.[5]

While all of those birds are impressive in flight, and the eagles are accomplished predators—California's skies produce sightings of creatures much larger—and much stranger—than any recognized by modern science.

Thunderbirds

Long before the first Europeans "discovered" the land they would christen America, aboriginal tribesmen lived in fear of "thunderbirds," huge raptors large enough to feed on men, elk—even small whales that were snatched from the ocean and dropped on dry land from great heights. California's Southern Miwok Indians, dwelling along the Merced River, called their resident thunderbirds *Yel'lo-kin.* Naturalist Clinton Hart Merriam (1855-1942), first chief of the U.S. Department of Agriculture's Division of Economic Ornithology and Mammalogy, described those giants in 1910.[6]

> "Yel'-lo-kin was a giant bird—the biggest bird in the world. He was in the habit of carrying off children—boys and girls up to fourteen or fifteen years of age. He took them by the top of the head and carried them up through the hole in the middle of the sky to his home on top of the sky, where he killed and ate them."[7]

Disregarding the mythic elements of that tradition, we are left with a fairly straightforward description of birds large enough to snatch adolescent human beings. Modern zoologists insist that condors and vultures are incapable of lifting any significant weight, while the lifting power of eagles depends on air speed. Biologist and falconer Ron Clarke explains: "On a wide-open beach, I have no doubt that an eagle with a full head of steam could pick up a six- or eight-pound dog and just keep on going. If it landed to kill a ten-pounder, and then tried to pick up and fly from a dead stop, could it get off the ground? Probably not."[8]

Witnesses report birds the size of small aircraft over California. *Courtesy of William Rebsamen*

Imagine, then, the size and speed required for a raptor to lift even a small child, weighing 30-50 pounds!

Do such giant birds exist in California? In the 1850s, San Francisco's *Daily Alta California* newspaper described an incident in which an unidentified bird with a 14-foot wingspan abducted a 9-pound pet rabbit. Frontiersman James Clyman (1792-1881) claimed several sightings of condors that size in the Golden State, but the unknown bird's hunting technique does not fit the condor's reputation as a scavenger.[9]

Reports of predatory thunderbirds in California persisted into the twentieth century, as revealed by author Jacques "Jack" Pearl (1923-92) in the May 1963 issue of *Saga* magazine. One witness cited by Pearl, an unnamed physician, was summoned from Ivanpah—now a Mojave Desert ghost town in San Bernardino County—to treat three injured members of a farmer's family in 1933. He arrived to find the farmer, his wife, and their three-year-old child badly cut, the adults relating a frightening tale.[10]

According to their story, the farmer was working his fields when he heard his wife screaming. Racing back to the house, he found her under attack by a "giant form of vulture or eagle" with 12-foot wings—a total estimated wingspan of some 25 feet. The lady defended herself with a fireplace poker, while the farmer grabbed an axe and flailed away, wounding the bird. Unfazed, it turned on him, gripped him with razor-sharp talons, and lifted him 10 feet into the air before dropping the farmer and flapping away. The doctor found marks of "tremendous bloodletting," far exceeding the blood loss suffered by his three patients.[11]

Eleven years later, another giant bird allegedly terrorized Nisei (Japanese-American) inmates of an World War II internment camp. Unfortunately, we are not told whether the supposed events occurred at Tule Lake (Siskiyou County) or Manzanar (in Owens Valley, northeast of Los Angeles). According to Jack Pearl, a half-dozen men disappeared from the camp over several months, in 1944, with those who remained insisting that a huge raptor had carried off the missing. Military guards were naturally skeptical, dismissing both the Nisei claims and an eyewitness report of one abduction offered by two Native American locals. Unlike other escapees from the country's 10 internment camps, however, none of those reported missing in this case were recaptured, and none returned to their families after the war.[12]

Jacques Pearl proposed that the birds in question were survivors of a prehistoric species, and today we know such giants *did* exist. They were the teratorns, large raptors that inhabited the Western Hemisphere during the Miocene and Pleistocene epochs, 23 million to

71

11,550 years ago. Distantly related to the modern condors, teratorns included the huge *Argentavis magnificens* (with a 26-foot wingspan, weighing 176 pounds), *Aiolornis incredibilis* (at 50 pounds, with a 16.5-foot wingspan), and *Teratornis merriami* (a 12.5-foot wingspan, 33 pounds). The last two species lived in California, while fossils of *Argentavis magnificens* have only been found in Argentina—but who can say how far its range extended?[13]

A reconstruction of a teratorn, the largest raptor known to science. *Courtesy of Michael Newton*

Most scientific texts describe teratorns as scavengers, like the condors and vultures, but their beaks bear a closer resemblance to those of hunting raptors, such as hawks and eagles. They also had longer and thicker legs than known vultures, suggesting that they could have stalked prey on the ground. *Argentavis* was large enough to swallow rabbit-sized prey in one gulp, and recent depictions of teratorns have deleted portrayal of bald heads and necks like the condor's.[14]

Raining Amphibians

Not every creature found in the strange skies of California flies. Some plummet to the ground from who-knows-where, like the peculiar creatures that bombarded Sacramento during summer 1879.

One morning in August, excited locals summoned the editor of the *Sacramento Reporter* to the city's west side, where they claimed that thousands of lizardlike creatures had fallen during a rainstorm. The editor confirmed that countless dark-brown quadrupeds, decorated with "bright spots" of unspecified color, were "moving animatedly" over a range of several blocks. Sacramento's opera house appeared to be ground zero for the living rain, with 200 of the unknown animals squirming in a single puddle outside. Their means of locomotion is uncertain, since the *Reporter* claimed that they "had no bones in their limbs." Indeed, they lost all energy when removed from water, and most of them died the following day, as downtown rain puddles evaporated.[15]

It seems that none of the wriggling things were preserved. Certainly, they were never formally identified. Some observers suggested that they were salamanders, present on the streets before the rain, but local residents could not have failed to see them in such numbers. Furthermore, the recent storm marked Sacramento's first rainfall in weeks, and since the unknown creatures died upon removal from the water, they could hardly have survived for long on sun-baked sidewalks.[16]

While the incident reported here appears to be California's only case of "living rain," strange showers are hardly unique. Author Charles Fort (1874-1932) catalogued many examples worldwide—including frogs, fish, alligators, and other live animals, along with flesh, blood, stones, etc.—from the early nineteenth century until his death. Such incidents continue, with a rain of cows over Siberia in 1990 and showers of unidentified slime in Tasmania during November 1996.[17]

Flying Reptiles

We have examined California's history of giant-snake sightings, but this report from February 1882 raises the mystery to new heights, with a multi-witness sighting of a serpent on the wing. Its great size and the fact that it could fly render it doubly mysterious.

According to the *Los Angeles Times,* the event occurred near Dos Palmas, in Riverside County, on the night of February 11. The story deserves to be quoted in full:

> One of the most startling snake stories that has been told in these parts for some time was related by the engineer and fireman who came in last night on the Southern Pacific express, and was corroborated by the passengers. It seems that just after the train had passed Dos Palms [*sic*], the engineer noticed, about half a mile ahead, what looked like a column of sand moving very slowly from east to west. At that time it was only a short distance from the track, and moving at such a pace that it was evident that train and column would come together. When the two monsters were but a short distance apart it was discovered that the column was not sand, but an animal of some kind.
>
> It was moving in almost a perpendicular position, the tail dragging on the ground and propelled by two large wings near the head. The bird, snake, or whatever it was, seemed to be about thirty feet long, and twelve inches in diameter. By this time everybody, almost, on the train, had put their heads out of the windows and were banging on the platform to get a better look at the monster snake. The train and snake came together, but the snake's tail was not where it should have been, and a portion of its lower extremities was clipped off. This seemed to put this flying snake on his mettle and he prepared for war. He wheeled around and gave chase to the flying train.
>
> The motion of the animal seemed to change in an instant, and he seemed to fly through the air two miles faster than chain lightning. In a few moments he, she or it, overtook the train, and began war after the latest snake style. The angry animal kept over the train and gave the train a lively thrashing, roaring like a cow in distress all the time. After breaking several windows and frightening the women and children almost to death, the monster called it off, followed by a shower of lead from the pistols of the passengers, which seemed to have no effect at all, if any of the bullets hit him. This is vouched for by every one who was on the train, and is given for what it is worth.[18]

Not much, perhaps, since some nineteenth-century newspapers hoaxed monster stories on slow news days—but the event was not unique. Before year's end, a pair of California lumberjacks reportedly observed a "flying crocodile" 18 feet long, sporting three pairs of wings and six pairs of legs. Sadly, no further details are available.[19]

The next report of strange flying reptiles emerged in July 1891, in the Selma *Enterprise.* It read:

Dragons in California

A number of persons living in the vicinity of Reedley, Fresno County, Cal., all reputable citizens, too, according to a Chronicle correspondent, swear that they have seen and hunted two dragons with wings fifteen feet long, bodies without covering of hair or feathers, head broad, bills long and wide, eyes not less than four inches in diameter, and with feet like those of an alligator somewhat, though more circular in form. They had five toes on each foot, with a strong claw on each, and its track is eleven inches wide and nineteen inches long. These strange creatures were first seen southeast of Selma, on the night of July 11, and their peculiar cries and the rustling of their mammoth wings were heard as late as 10 o'clock, when all became still. The dragons were last heard that night crying in the direction of King's river.

Two nights later, A.X. Simmons's poultry yard was visited by the monsters, many of the hens being bitten in two and left partly devoured. Those who examined the dead chickens say the teeth marks on them resemble those made by a very large dog. On July 19 a carriage loaded with picnickers was returning from a picnic on Clark's bridge, and in the clear moonlight saw the monsters plainly circling in the air and heard the rush of their pinions, snapping of their jaws and fearful cries overhead. On Monday, July 21, Harvey Lemon and Major Henry Haight, who live just outside of Selma, going after their hogs, who fed on the tules, heard a strangling noise in the deep swale under a bridge, and in a moment, with a heavy flapping of wings, the queer creatures rose slowly from the water, flying so close to the men that the wind from the tremendous wings was plainly felt. Their description of the monsters tallies with that of the persons who saw them on the 13th and 19th.[20]

Did pterodactyls visit Selma in 1891? *Courtesy of William Rebsamen*

A subsequent report, published in Ohio's *Salem Daily News* on October 24, 1891, reports that: "After they had made several appearances, a party was organized to hunt them. One of them was wounded and tracked several miles and his track in the mud secured."[21]

Researcher Chad Arment, to whom we owe the resurrection of these articles, has also unearthed stories from the *Fresno Bee*, the *Fresno Weekly Republican*, and the Oakland *Tribune* which dismiss the entire affair as a hoax fueled by liquor—yet Arment admits the possibility that the initial sightings may have involved misidentification of a known bird species.[22]

Science does recognize some "flying" reptiles, although none of them have wings or truly fly, as do bats and birds. Snakes of the genus *Chrysopelea*, including five mildly-venomous Asian species, flatten their bodies while springing and gliding from tree to tree. Likewise, lizards of the genus *Draco*—29 species in all—glide through Asian forests with the aid of membranes attached to their ribs. The largest species, *Draco volans* ("flying dragon") rarely exceeds nine inches in length, and could hardly be mistaken for a pterodactyl, even if one found its way to California in the 1890s.[23]

A Flying Man

Our next case does not properly involve a "monster," but it rates inclusion here for sheer peculiarity. Vern Morse, a 20-year policeman, was returning home to San Francisco with his wife, around 11:00 p.m. on December 3, 1966, when they saw a strange object airborne above Bayshore Freeway, south of San Jose.[24]

"At first," Morse later told reporters, "it looked like a parachute flare. I thought that it would land in those buildings east of the Southern Pacific Depot and start a fire. When it crossed the highway directly in front of me, it stopped descending at an altitude of about 200 feet and started climbing. My wife said, 'Somebody's guiding it.'"[25]

Morse parked his car at a closed service station to watch the flying object more safely. On closer examination, it appeared to be a glowing cylinder, some eight or nine feet long and three feet in diameter.[26]

As Morse explained, "What had first appeared to be parachute shroud lines were plainly struts connecting the solid lower portion of the cylinder with the upper portion which was topped by a nose cone resembling a crash helmet. It looked like a flying platform with somebody standing up inside it. It passed over at about 300 or 400 feet and it didn't make a sound."[27]

Another motorist also saw the "flying birdcage" and its occupant, proceeding toward Bay Meadows Race Track. As it soared over the track, Morse said, "The light on it went out, just as if somebody had turned a switch."[28]

Who was the strange airman? Did Morse and company observe some new, experimental aircraft still unrevealed to the public, for whatever reason? The mystery remains unsolved.

Flying Apes?

Our last flying cryptids reside, oddly enough, in the files of the International Bigfoot Society. The IBS assigns two case numbers to the events, while stressing that there were actually *three* individual reports, all collected by researcher Peter Gutilla.[29]

According to Gutilla, the reports issued "from precipitous regions southeast of Mt. Baldy" (in San Bernardino County), comprising three encounters with "a leaping, dog-faced, hairy-winged creature that left behind wide, 18-inch three-toed footprints." No dates or other details are provided, but Gutilla links those sightings to the July 1994 discovery of large three-toed tracks near Upland and Cucamonga Wash in the same county. The following year, both three- and five-toed tracks were found in the same area. And there, sadly, the matter rests...at least, for now.[30]

Chapter 5

The Alien Big Cats (ABCs)

Science does not define "big cats" by size. Rather, the formal designation is reserved for felids that possess a specially-adapted larynx and hyoid apparatus which permits them to roar. Only members of the genus *Panthera*—including the lion, tiger, leopard, and jaguar—thus qualify scientifically as big (or "great") cats. Some authors include two other large species—the cougar and snow leopard—on lists of big cats, though neither technically qualifies.[1]

Scientifically speaking, the Western Hemisphere's only big cat is the jaguar (*Panthera onca*). Once found across much of the southern United States, southward through Mexico, Central America, and South America, jaguars have been virtually extirpated from U.S. soil. A single specimen, identified by its unique rosettes, was photographed in Arizona on three occasions, between 2001 and 2004, while a sighting from New Mexico in March 2006 remains unconfirmed. Meanwhile, in January 2008, the U.S. Fish and Wildlife Service abandoned its jaguar recovery program under the Endangered Species Act, the first such move in 34 years. Critics accused President George Bush of sacrificing the species for his plans to build a giant fence along the Mexican border.[2]

Cryptozoologists are less rigorous in defining what they call "alien big cats"—or ABCs, for short. Ignoring physiology, they apply the label to any large felid reported from locations where it should not exist in the wild—either because it has been extirpated (like the jaguar or the Eastern cougar), or because it is not native to the region. Thus, a cougar found in England or Australia qualifies for ABC status, while those inhabiting the western U.S. and southern Florida do not. Lions, leopards, and tigers found outside captivity in North America are likewise ABCs.[3]

Cougars

As noted, cougars (*Puma concolor*) are native to California. In fact, their historical range is the greatest of any wild terrestrial mammal in the Western Hemisphere, extending from the Yukon in Canada to the southern Andes in South America. In North America, that range once spread from sea to sea, but habitat destruction and unrestricted hunting drove the species to presumed extinction east of the Mississippi River, by the early 1900s. Cougars—also known as pumas, mountain lions, catamounts, and panthers—are the New World's second-heaviest cats (after jaguars), and the world's fourth-heaviest.[4]

The cougar is America's largest known cat. *Courtesy of US Fish & Wildlife Service*

Despite their size and predatory prowess, cougars pose little danger to humans. Only 108 confirmed attacks have been recorded in North America since 1890, resulting in 20 human fatalities. Curiously, 50 of those cases have occurred since 1991, as civilization continues its encroachment on wild habitats. California, with an estimated 5,000 cougars at large in 2008, recorded only three attacks between 1890 and 1985, while a dozen more (with three fatalities) have occurred since 1986.[5]

Cougars impinge on our review of California ABCs for two reasons: first, because a witness unfamiliar with the species might mistake a cougar for a female lion (*Panthera leo*); and second, because hypothetical melanistic cougars may account for reports of "black panthers" at large. That said, we leave them for the moment to address the Golden State's first ABC, which bears no resemblance at all to a native species.

Tiger, Tiger

Lake County, north of San Francisco Bay, was barely seven years old in spring 1868, when a ferocious predator terrorized local ranchers, savaging their sheep and colts. Resident Archie McGrath described the incidents and the slayer in his memoirs, collected by Ellery and Marie Sleeper for the county's centennial in 1961. McGrath described the slaughter thus:

"As we were going along we found the ground all torn up under a tree and saw where a horse had run down hill. We followed the tracks and could see that something was wrong. We followed for about a quarter of a mile and found a dead horse. He had been killed by a California Lion. The horse was a large three-year and weighed about twelve hundred pounds. He was a Clidesdale [sic] and large for his age. Not far from there we found where the lion had killed a large two-year old colt of the same stock. They had been opened and their entrails were cleaned out as nice as a butcher could have done with his knife."[6]

Two days later, McGrath "came to several bunches of sheep that a lion had killed and carried together. There were ten or twelve in each bunch. I counted over forty that the lion had killed during the two nights I had left the sheep alone."[7]

McGrath penned his surviving sheep that night, then released them in the morning, but they soon came running back in a state of panic. He then released his dogs to track the beast, and later wrote:

"They treed the lion before they had run a half-mile. The lion had killed a half grown lamb and skinned it and taken the entrails out.

"When I was within seventy yards of the tree where the dogs had the lion treed, I was out of breath and tired so I stopped to rest and get my wind. The lion was in a large fir tree about fifty feet high. After I was rested, I worked around to the upper side of the tree; he had his legs around the trunk of the tree with his back to the limb and would look first to one side of the tree then the other to see what was going on. When he saw me he got up to jump. He was too quick for me. I raised my gun to shoot just as he jumped so I missed him; but when he hit the ground the dogs did not give him time to climb another tree. The lion would reach out and grab a dog but the others would fight so hard he could not hurt the dog before he would have to let him up to fight off the others. I finally got up to a tree and waited until I have a chance to shoot and not hit a dog. I finally shot the lion in the head and killed him.

"He was the largest one ever killed in that country, weighing over three hundred pounds and measuring eleven feet from the tip of his nose to the tip of his tail. I had to get George to help me get the lion on a saddle horse and his feet touched the ground on both sides. I have killed many panthers and what they call California lions, but this was the only California lion that I have ever seen in those mountains. It was built entirely different from a panther, it was very heavy in front and light behind with black stripes along its shoulders and back and down the fore parts. The rest was of a yellow cast color. The black was on his back and shoulders and it resembled a mane. The hair was longer there.[8]

While fascinating in itself, for the detailed description of this still-unidentified ABC, McGrath's report is more significant for its separation of "California lions" from "panthers"—which can only be cougars. McGrath and his contemporaries clearly distinguished between the two species, and McGrath himself claims to have killed "many" specimens, the latest merely qualifying as his largest trophy. Curiously, all other reports of "California lions" presently accessible clearly refer to cougars, like the eight-foot, 250-pound specimen shot in Mariposa County, in November 1854, and the cat that attacked John Day near Steiner Flat (Trinity County) in February 1873.[9]

Was McGrath simply confused, or did another species still unknown to science coexist with California cougars in the nineteenth century? Without the hide or other remnants of his kill, which were apparently discarded, we may never know. McGrath's "lion," however, would not be the last large striped cat to frighten California residents.

Ventura County, northwest of Los Angeles, experienced a rash of ABC sightings in February 2005. The furor began on February 8, when residents of Simi Valley found feline paw prints measuring six inches wide. A week later, farmhand Louis Romo glimpsed a large cat slinking through shrubbery on the Day Creek Ranch, near the Ronald Reagan Presidential Library. "It scared me," Rolo told reporters. "It was amazing." Authorities found more tracks at the ranch, which matched those found on February 8. Two days after that discovery, spokesmen for the California Fish and Game Department warned that an exotic cat was at large between Moorpark and Simi Valley.[10]

But what kind of cat? Experts opined that the paw marks suggested a felid weighing 400-600 pounds, three to four times the size of a normal cougar. Fish and Game's Lieutenant Chris Long told journalists, "The reported color of the animal was tan or brown. There were no spots or stripes seen on the body." Speculation therefore focused on a lion, but the beast remained elusive. A tracker employed by California's Department of Agriculture found more prints on February 18, but opined that they were several days old. A sheriff's helicopter joined the search on February 19, and more tracks were found that day on the west side of Highway 23, near Thousand Oaks. Police warned parents not to leave their children unattended.[11]

Large striped cats have been seen in California since 1868.
Courtesy of US Fish & Wildlife Service

Nearly everyone assumed the cat was an escaped exotic pet. Indeed, Romo's sighting came just three days after Abby and Emma Hendregan removed 22 exotic cats—including lions, tigers, and lynxes—from their Moorpark property on Lapeyre Road, in Tierra Rejada Valley. Authorities said their beasts were improperly caged, but the stray cat was not one of theirs, as Lieutenant Long confirmed.

"All the animals were accounted for when they were removed," he said. "We are investigating any missing cats in the time prior to the Lapeyre incident."[12]

But none were found. No negligent amateur zookeepers surfaced. And the search went on. Traps baited with chickens failed to attract the huge prowler. Airborne infrared cameras searched in vain for traces of its body heat. A "sighting" near the Reagan Library, on February 21, led riflemen to surround a boulder.[13]

The search expanded on February 22, as five two-person teams—each consisting of a state game warden and a tracker from the U.S. Department of Agriculture—moved westward toward Leisure Village, in Camarillo. The end came one day later, with a flurry of gunfire in Moorpark, as hunters shot and killed their prey. The shoot-to-kill decision sprang from fears that tranquilizer darts might act too slowly to prevent the cat from fleeing once again.[14]

And, yes, despite Chris Long's announcement to the media five days earlier, the dead cat *was* a tiger with a clearly-recognizable striped coat. "It's unfortunate that we had to kill it," Fish and Game spokesperson Lorna Bernard told the media. "It's even more unfortunate that the person who owned it didn't come forward and alert us immediately. We might have been able to capture it."[15]

Perhaps, and yet the hypothetical scofflaw remains unidentified today, despite an exhaustive canvass of all Californians licensed to own exotic cats.[16] And one year later, almost to the day, another free-roaming tiger grabbed headlines in southern California.

Valley Center is located in San Diego County, 29 miles northeast of downtown San Diego proper. Its celebrity residents, past and present, include John Wayne and Gary Cooper, Dick Powell and June Allyson, Fred Astaire, Bill Murray, Steve Reeves, NFL placekicker Billy Cundiff, and Glenn Bell (founder of Taco Bell).[17] And in the second week of February 2006, it had a most unwelcome visitor.

At 10 a.m. on February 11, Valley Center firefighters received the first telephone report of a large tiger roaming the neighborhood of Carney and McNally Roads. Two more calls followed, estimating the cat's weight at 500 pounds and reporting that it wore a collar. The fire department—which sometimes rescues cats from trees, but does not wrangle tigers—relayed those calls to the sheriff's office, which in turn notified the California Department of Forestry, charged with control of wild animals.[18]

As in Simi Valley the previous year, police teamed with game wardens to sweep the countryside, assisted by airborne spotters. This time, however, they did not find their prey. The tiger vanished as mysteriously as it had appeared, and was not seen again.[19]

The King of Beasts

Archie McGrath's ABC of 1868 may not have been a lion, but an apparent specimen of *Panthera leo* did visit northern California a century later, in November 1979. Eyewitnesses agreed on the beast's identity, but they proved less adept than McGrath at tracking it down.

The scene was Fremont, in Alameda County. Founded as a Spanish mission 1797 and named for "Great Pathfinder" John C. Frémont in 1846, the city was incorporated in January 1956, to merge five smaller towns. Cougars are not unknown in the vicinity, but Old World lions theoretically do not exist outside of zoos in San Francisco, San Jose, Oakland and Santa Rosa.[20]

All of the cats within those institutions were accounted for between 5:27 and 6:28 p.m. on November 10, 1979, when residents around Coyote Hills Regional Park called authorities to report an adult male lion roaming free along Alameda Creek. Witnesses pegged the cat's weight between 300 and 400 pounds, noting that its roars could be heard over several blocks around Alvarado Boulevard.[21]

Forty-odd searchers turned out to hunt the lion, including animal control officers, police, firefighters, and employees of the East Bay Regional Park District. Tracking dogs joined the search, augmented by a helicopter on loan from the Bay Area Rapid Transit District. At 9:00 p.m., Fremont Patrolman William Fontes met the cat beneath a Nimitz Freeway overpass (now Interstate 880). Blinded by the officer's flashlight, the lion snarled, then turned and fled. It was last seen near the Turk Island Landfill, west of Fremont on Union City Boulevard, shortly before searchers called off their hunt at 10:00 p.m. One of the trackers, Coyote Hills Regional Park maintenance supervisor Charles Johnson, told reporters, "They didn't check that underbrush while I was there. They just flew the helicopter over it and turned on sirens to scare the lion."[22]

Apparently, it worked. The lion was not seen again, and some locals were amused when the owner of a 40-pound chow puppy claimed his dog had been the animal in question. Patrolman Fontes categorically denied it, saying, "The puppy in no way resembled the 300 to 400 pound animal observed in the flood control channel." Karen Burhardt, an expert in animal tracks from Marine World/Africa USA in Redwood Shores, confirmed that tracks left by the lion were those of "a large cat," but their maker had vanished forever.[23]

Lions prowled California during 1979-83. *Courtesy of US National Oceanic and Atmospheric Administration*

Another maned lion surfaced in October 1983, this time at El Toro, 363 miles south of Fremont, in conservative Orange County. Once again, authorities turned out to track the cat. And once again, they searched in vain. The king of beasts eluded them and disappeared.[24]

"Black Panthers"

Scientifically speaking, there is no such thing as a "black panther." That term is normally applied to melanistic (black) leopards or jaguars, while albino or leucistic members of the same species are sometimes called "white panthers." Cougars are also known as panthers in parts of North America—particularly Florida—and while some persons claim to have seen or killed black cougars, no melanistic specimen has been formally documented.[25]

Leopards are Old World cats, native to Africa and Asia. Jaguars, while indigenous to the New World, have been virtually exterminated from North America. Neither of the two specimens reported from the southwestern United States during 2001-06 was melanistic. And yet, black panther sightings are reported across the country, from coast to coast and border to border.

California's "panther" sightings date from September 1964, when San Rafael's *Marin Independent Journal* reported a large black cat prowling around Marin County, north of San Francisco. The ink was barely dry on those reports when the action shifted to Ventura County, 300 miles to the south. There, in the Conejo Valley, *two* black panthers were seen, roaming together, but hunters failed to locate them.[26]

A lone panther returned to Ventura County on December 12, 1967, startling four workmen at the county sewage plant. Sheriff's deputies answered the call and saw the cat, but their car plunged into a pool of sewage and sank, while the panther escaped. Twelve days later, a member of the U.S. Air Force went panther-hunting in his spare time and stranded himself on a 600-foot cliff face, requiring a team of rescuers to save him. The Ventura County panther made its last appearance on January 9, 1968, appearing to Kenneth French and his wife, but once again eluding police.[27]

Spring 1972 produced a panther "flap" in Contra Costa County, east of Oakland. Gary Bogue, then curator of Walnut Creek's Alexander Lindsey Jr. Museum, received two calls within three days from witnesses reporting black panther sightings. The first caller watched the cat through binoculars, during his lunch break at home. The second—who had never met the first—was walking his dog with a 5-foot-long panther leaped from a nearby tree and ran into the woods. Three weeks later and 12 miles away, two residents saw a panther chasing cattle, then pausing to drink from a backyard swimming pool. A month after that incident, U.S. Navy personnel and animal control officers chased a black panther around the Concord Naval Weapons Depot but failed to capture it.[28]

Panthers haunted Contra Costa County through year's end. In autumn 1972 a farmer near Mount Diablo complained that ducks and geese had vanished from his property, while his wife heard purring like the sound of a huge cat beneath their bedroom window. One night, when his horses squealed in panic and the family's German shepherd scratched frantically at the back door, the farmer rushed outside with a flashlight, in time to see a panther ambling away. It left paw prints five inches wide.[29]

Three months after that incident, in the final days of 1972, two cats surprised a naturalist at Las Trampas Regional Wilderness, a 5,342-acre park shared by Alameda and Contra Costa Counties. According to that expert witness, the cats—which he saw chasing deer—included a black panther *and* a normal tawny-colored cougar.[30]

"Black panthers" are melanistic jaguars or leopards.
Courtesy of William Rebsamen

A large black cat next surfaced in the town of San Jose, 46 miles south of Concord, in December 1973. Thomas Mantei, a navy lieutenant commander, reported that his collie had pursued the cat and treed it in a eucalyptus near his home, but it escaped once more. On December 19, Larry Rephahn of Fremont—16 miles above San Jose, in Yolo County—told police that he had nearly struck a panther with his car, as it crossed Niles Canyon Road near Joyland Park.[31]

Black panthers took their leave of California for 11 years after the Fremont incident, then returned to appear in San Dimas—333 miles farther south, in Los Angeles County—on May 20, 1984. Searches proved futile there, and in Fairfield (Solano County, 371 miles north of San Dimas), where witnesses saw another black cat on April 9, 1988.[32]

California panther sightings continue in the twenty-first century, centered on the same Las Trampas Regional Wilderness where a black cat and a cougar were seen hunting in tandem, three decades earlier. Two separate hikers reported sightings in October 2004, prompting Steve Bobzian, a cougar expert with the East Bay Regional Park District, to admit, "We're getting at least one or two black panther sightings a year." Journalist Tom Stienstra, investigating for the *San Francisco Chronicle,* uncovered sightings at Sunol Regional Wilderness (Alameda County), Anthony Chabot Regional Park (in Oakland), Carquinez Strait Regional Shoreline (on San Pablo Bay), and the Marin Headlands (Marin County, above the Golden Gate). Farther south, records disclosed sightings near San Louis Obispo and at Lake Arrowhead, in San Bernardino County.[33]

In April 2008, Stienstra reported another black panther sighting—this one claimed by outdoorsman John Balawejder at Point Reyes National Seashore. Balawejder knows cougars, having seen nearly a dozen on his frequent nature hikes, and claimed the latest felid on his list was a melanistic cougar. As he described the incident, "We came up a short rise through a grassy swale, and then, looking up, saw a large, jet-black mountain lion calmly sitting, eyes half asleep looking out at us from about 30 yards away. My friend and I stood there, stunned. It then started to slink away from us in a large semi-circle, attempting to hide in the grass. This lion was not darkish, not a brownish-tawny like some I've seen since, but jet black."[34]

The following month, Don Callen released three photos of a large black cat prowling his 52-acre property near Forestville, in Sonoma County. Callen described the animal, photographed on March 13 and again on April 5, as standing thigh-high to a man, but experts who viewed the photos—including Jack Dumbacher, a curator at the California Academy of Sciences in San Francisco, and Rob Dicely, owner of an exotic cat preserve with 19 inmates at Occidental—

deemed the pictures inconclusive. Dicely said that "it could be" a black cougar, then suggested a black house cat or melanistic bobcat, noting that some cougars have dark-brown coats which may "easily be mistaken for black."[35]

Another rash of Bay Area panther sightings erupted in autumn 2008. Michaela Graham of Richmond logged two encounters in Miller-Knox Park, near her home, describing the beast as "a big black cat, no housecat, but a large cat. Jet black, no other colors." Larz Sherer was hiking through Castro Valley, near Redwood Road, when he a met a black felid resembling the "sort of animal [that] should be in Africa, not the East Bay." John Balawejder and Burke Richardson were near Tomales Point, in the Point Reyes National Seashore, when they saw "a large, jet-black mountain lion calmly sitting, eyes half asleep looking out at us from about 30 yards away."[36]

What Are They?

Multiple explanations are advanced for black panther sightings in North America. Melanistic cougars seem most popular, though none has yet been scientifically confirmed by means of specimens or hides procured from anywhere on Earth. George-Louis Leclerc, in his *Histoire Naturelle* (1749), published the first description of black cougars in South America, but it appears that he confused them with melanistic jaguars. Author Jerry Coleman (brother of Loren) examined a supposed black cougar, stuffed and mounted on an Indian reservation at Cherokee, North Carolina, and exposed it as a cat shot in Montana, whose fur was later dyed black. Steve Torres, speaking for California's Department of Fish and Game, offered the state's opinion on black cougars in November 2004: "They say it's a black color morph of a mountain lion, and biologically there is always the possibility that they're out there. More likely, they are seeing something else." Steve Bobsian, a wildlife biologist with the East Bay Regional Park District, agrees, noting that California has more than 12,000 confirmed cougar sightings on file. "If you look at all the pelts that are out there," he told the *San Francisco Chronicle,* "nobody has even one mountain lion pelt that looks black."[37]

But *what?*

Some researchers suggest that North American black panthers—at least in the Southwest—may be melanistic jaguars. Science rejects that possibility, as well, noting that jaguars have been extirpated from most of the United States, and that the only confirmed specimen sighted in recent years displayed a normal spotted coat. No mainstream scientist presently supports the notion of a jaguar breeding colony in California, much less *black* jaguars.[38]

Black leopards are another possibility, and would be doubly strange if found at large in California, breeding in the wild. Given the frequency of black panther sightings in America—1,345 reports from 25 eastern states since 1950; 330 from Pennsylvania alone—it seems unlikely that all incidents can be explained in terms of exotic pet owners releasing or losing their cats. One innovative theory, published online, suggests that black leopards may have arrived in the U.S. as mascots aboard antebellum slave ships, and may have escaped to breed in the wild. While intriguing, that theory is presently unsupported by any historical evidence.[39]

The other common claims, that panther witnesses have merely seen black bobcats or house cats, fail on account of size. Black bobcats *do* exist, but they average three feet in length (versus the cats described as four to six feet long) and normally weigh twenty pounds (against eyewitness estimates of panthers weighing 100-150 pounds). More critically, the stubby tail that gives bobcats their name bears no resemblance to the long tails normally seen on California's elusive panthers. House cats, meanwhile, may deceive the occasional frightened witness or feature in some fuzzy "panther" photographs, but no sober witness could confuse a domestic cat with a panther at close range.[40]

Authors Loren Coleman and Mark Hall propose the most surprising explanation for North American black panthers *and* lions at large. Specifically, they suggest that specimens of *Panthera leo atrox*—the American lion or cave lion—did not become extinct 10,000 years ago, as commonly believed, but have survived to the present day. Stranger still, Coleman and Hall suggest a high incidence of sexual dimorphism within the Pleistocene species, producing maned male adults resembling (but larger than) modern lions, while melanistic females appear as black panthers. This theory has the added benefit of explaining incidents where lions and panthers have been seen together in modern times —but, it must be said, no scientific evidence currently supports either survival of *P. l. atrox,* or the claim that females displayed black pellage. In fact, most paleontologists agree that male cave lions either had small manes, or none at all.[41]

Some researchers believe that prehistoric cave lions still exist in North America. *Courtesy of Michael Newton*

Chapter 6

Wild Woodsmen

California is Bigfoot country. Reports of large unknown bipedal creatures, also known as Sasquatch, span four centuries and number in the hundreds. In fact, so many eyewitness encounters and discoveries of huge humanoid footprints have been logged over the years, that hopeless confusion surrounds the statistical record.

In illustration of this point, we note that Canadian researcher John Green, writing in 1977, claimed 343 California Bigfoot sightings on file; Christopher Murphy cites the same total for 2006, as if no sightings had occurred during the intervening 30 years. Authors Colin and Janet Bord list 114 cases between the 1850s and 2006. An atlas published by the U.S. Army Corps of Engineers in 1975 cites 151 cases statewide. The Bigfoot Field Researchers Organization (BFRO) claims 379 California cases, but five are duplicated on the group's website, while a sixth is cross-referenced but not counted. The Gulf Coast Bigfoot Research Organization (GCBRO) website lists only 25 sightings from the Golden State, but its focus lies elsewhere. The International Bigfoot Society (IBS) claims 433 sightings, but elimination of duplicates and references to vague legends reduces that tally to 357. Many of the cases listed in those sources—54 percent in the Army tabulation—involve discovery of footprints, reports of strange noises or smells, without actual sightings of Bigfoot.[1]

My own tally, admittedly conservative and drawn from all the sources named above—plus various media reports—includes 566 Bigfoot sightings or presumed encounters for the state at large, from the late eighteenth century through 2007.

California is Bigfoot country.
Courtesy of William Rebsamen

Bigfoot in Prehistory

Long before Canadian journalist J.W. Burns coined the "Indian" term *Sasquatch* in 1929, before California reporters first printed the "Bigfoot" nickname in 1958, Native Americans knew the Pacific Northwest's forest-dwelling giants by a wide variety of names, including *chihalenchi, loo poo oyes* and *toké-mussi* among Miwoks in northern California; *madukarahat,* among the Karoks; *miitiipi* ("disaster") among Kaiwaiisu in the Mojave Desert; *oh-mah* ("demon" or "wild man") among the Hupas and Yuroks; *olayome* ("rock people") among the Pomos at Clear Lake; *tah-tah-kle'-ah* among the Yakima; *takwis* or *towis* ("devil") among Gabrielenos on the Santa Ana River; and as *tso'apittse* ("cannibal giant") among the Shoshoni.[2]

The first "white" explorers of California were Spaniards, arriving in 1542. Spanish priests established their first California mission at San Diego, in 1769, and one year later logged the earliest Western report of large unknown bipeds in North America. Based on interrogation of Gabrieleno tribesmen, the padres determined that local natives lived in fear of hairy "devils" who prowled by night and emitted foul odors. So numerous were the savage wildmen, in fact, that a plot on the Santa Ana River's southern bank was called *towis puki,* "camp of the devil." Another district, in present-day Los Angeles County, between the modern cities of La Verne and Pomona, was dubbed *Toybipet,* or "devil woman who was there." In Riverside County, hairy monsters were said to inhabit a cave on Lily Rock (west of Palm Springs), San Jacinto Peak. and Tahquitz Peak, which is named for the "devils."[3]

The Nineteenth Century

Recitation of native legends gave way to sightings by Anglo-European settlers after California's gold rush hastened statehood in 1850, producing 14 claims of meetings with unknown primates by the end of the nineteenth century. Mount Shasta claimed the first eyewitness report, sometime in the 1850s, but it was not publicized until March 1960, when John Weekes wrote a letter to *TRUE Magazine,* in response to a story on Bigfoot. That letter read:

"My grandfather prospected for gold in the eighteen fifties throughout the region described as being home of the Snowman. Upon grandfather's return to the East, he told stories of seeing hairy giants in the vicinity of Mount Shasta. These monsters had long arms, but short legs. One of them picked up a 20-foot section of sluiceway and smashed it to bits against a tree."[4]

Deadman Hole, located near Holcomb Village in northern San Diego County, first earned its lethal reputation as a watering hole for coaches of the Stage Line, launched in September 1858. One afternoon, before year's end, a driver stopping to water his horses found a human corpse adrift in the natural pool. Twelve years later, a French shepherd was slain on the site, and in 1876 a stagecoach passenger reported seeing a naked, hairy "thing" in the bushes nearby. William Blair, found strangled at Deadman Hole "a few years later," had influential friends in San Francisco, but their investigation of the crime proved fruitless. An Indian woman died in that same unspecified year, throttled within 200 feet of the Blair murder scene. Two local hunters, Charles Cox and Edward Dean, braved the canyon in March 1888, allegedly killing an unknown creature that resembled a gorilla, but which had an "Indian face," with long fangs like a bear's. A local newspaper, the *Daily Transcript,* claimed the monster was transported by wagon to San Diego, for public exhibition, but it apparently vanished into thin air.[5]

Four hundred miles to the north, near Orestimba Creek in Stanislaus County, a hunter met two mysterious primates in autumn 1869. Time after time, the man found ashes from his campfire scattered, though his gear was not disturbed. At last, he lay in wait to catch the prowler, with astonishing results. As he wrote to the Antioch *Ledger,* in October 1870:

> "I was never so benumbed with astonishment before. The creature, whatever it was, stood fully five feet high, and disproportionately broad and square at the fore shoulders, with arms of great length. The legs were very short and the body long. The head was small compared with the rest of the creature, and appeared to be set upon his shoulders without a neck. The whole was covered with dark brown and cinnamon colored hair, quite long in some parts, that on the head standing in a shock and growing close to the eyes, like a Digger Indian's."[6]

The hunter resisted an impulse to shoot, watching as the creature grabbed smoking sticks from the fire and swung them around its head. After 15 minutes, the beast whistled and was answered by another—"a female, unmistakably"—with which it disappeared into the woods.[7]

A month before the *Ledger* published that report, in September 1870, two other hunters reported seeing "gorillas" near Orestimba Creek. That same month, the San Joaquin *Republican* reported that a "wild man" had been seen near Mount Diablo, in Contra Costa County. Its footprints measured 13 inches long.[8]

In April 1876, the San Diego *Union* reported Turner Helm's encounter with a "missing link" near Warner's Ranch. Despite a full-body coat of dark hair like a bear's, Helm noted that the beast had "rather fine features—not at all like those of an Indian, but more like an American or Spaniard."[9]

Six years elapsed before the next rash of sightings, from Inyo County, in early 1882. Three hunters tracked the "large, shaggy beast" on March 25, and Jack Ferral allegedly shot it five times before his horse bolted, breaking two legs in its panic. The unknown beast escaped, apparently unharmed.[10]

Four years later, on January 2, 1886, the Del Norte *Record* reported Jack Dover's sighting of a 7-foot-tall biped "with a bull dog head, short ears and long hair." Dover refrained from firing on the beast "because it was so human." Even more astounding was the creature seen by John Forsee near Mount Dana (Mono County), in April 1890. It wore coyote skins and "round Indian snowshoes," and seemed "agile as a deer."[11]

By contrast, the creature seen near Rumsey (Yolo County) in April 1891 was "some kind of monstrosity, which snatched game from a hunter's bag, snapped large branches from trees "as if they were toothpicks," and wielded them as clubs against the hunter's dogs before it fled. Local farmers blamed it for the disappearance of their hogs and sheep.[12]

August 1893 brought reports from Fresno of the "Jabberwock," which "resembles a human being, beats his breast with his long, powerful arms, and gives utterance to loud, guttural roars that make the air shiver as well as the spectators." Three years later, at Eureka, Jake McCoy and L.T. Mills smelled an "awful stench" like rotting flesh, then saw a manlike figure "covered with dark hair and long like the mane of a horse." A similar stench accompanied the creature that took fish from witness Tawani Wakawa in summer 1897. Unfortunately, California has 13 Tule Lakes in 10 counties, rendering the incident untraceable.[13]

1900-1957

The first half of the twentieth century offers 30 alleged Bigfoot encounters. Of those, 26 are eyewitness sightings, while three describe peripheral events and one refers to an elusive (possibly mythical) photograph.

Sightings were sparse during the first two decades of the century, with only two on record. Witness Tawani Wakawa, from the 1897 episode, claimed that a 9-foot biped treated him for snakebite, then carried him back to his Mount Shasta campsite in 1901. Seven years later, a shaggy "half-human beast" robbed trappers of their prey in the Santa Monica Mountains.[14]

The IBS website claims that hunters tracked "red-haired wildmen" around Pyramid Lake in the 1920s and 1930s, but the site places that lake in Lake County, while California's two lakes of that name are actually found in El Dorado and Los Angeles Counties. Another vague report describes a hairy "woodsman" crossing the road between Albion and Willits (Mendocino County), sometime in the 1930s.[15]

A more specific case, from 1934, involves large humanoid tracks found by a man named Zebo, near Mount Bally in Humboldt County. Zebo photographed the "single line" of footprints, but his photos have never been published.[16]

Five years later, in Orange County's Borrego Canyon, a camper was approached by several light-haired bipeds with glowing red eyes, one night in 1939. The witness thought the creatures planned to kill his burro, but his fire kept them at bay.[17]

The 1940s produced muddled data, including six eyewitness sightings and two more dubious cases. In 1940, a brown-haired, 7-foot biped relieved two Plumas County hunters of a deer they had shot in the Genesee Valley. Four years later, in August 1944, Margaret Whitney and her brother saw three flat-faced primates ranging from five to seven feet tall, walking along McKinney Creek in Siskiyou County. In spring 1947, two motorists saw an 8- or 9-foot reddish-haired primate cross Highway 99, south of Shasta. That May, Russ Tribble and his wife saw two smelly primates eating fish and reeds near Fall River Mills (Shasta County). A witness known only as "Granny" claimed a sighting near the Trinity River, in 1948. Finally, a Mendocino County witness saw Bigfoot carrying an armload of fish near Fort Bragg, but could recall no date beyond "the 1940s."[18]

The decade's other incidents are vague, at best. Witness J.W. Rowland claimed that an unseen, foul-smelling prowler "rattled" a decrepit cabin near Onion Lake (Humboldt County) sometime in the 1940s, while a Yreka resident claimed memories of newspaper photo published in 1943 or 1949, depicting "a group of men with a Bigfoot in chains." Needless to say, the photo remains elusive.[19]

Bigfoot would burst upon America and the world full-force in 1958, but the creature's appearances during 1950-57 excited only local comment. Solitary primates visited Humboldt and San Bernardino Counties in 1950, the former wearing tattered clothes, while a "family" of three appeared near Ojai, in Ventura County. The tallest was about 5 feet 4 inches tall, its companions 3.5 feet tall. All three displayed "kind of Negroid" features.[20]

Vaguely dated incidents from 1951-53 include a child's campground sighting from Tuolumne County, reports of a "Speedway Monster" at Fontana, a nocturnal sighting near Lewiston (Trinity County), and the frightening tale of a logger who was stalked by a 6-foot biped near Orleans, in Humboldt County.[21]

The year 1954 produced three alleged sightings, but two are now suspect, having been logged and researched by notorious hoaxer Ray Wallace. Wallace's stories came (he said) from loggers in Del Norte and Humboldt Counties, the latter case involving bipeds that carried large clubs and robbed timber-cutters of their lunches. The third account, from witness Martin Witter, describes his meeting with "a stump that moved" near Mount Tallac, in El Dorado County.[22]

The action shifted to Tulare County in August 1955, with a nocturnal sighting of a 7-foot creature whose head resembled "a diver bell helmet." A year later, "Ted from Carson City" shot a Bigfoot in the head with his .30-30 rifle, 10 miles east of Redding, but the beast escaped. That autumn, three hunters saw a biped 8-9 feet tall, near Truckee (Nevada County), but held their fire. In Kneeland (Humboldt County), during summer 1957, three children met a 7-foot creature on Ole Hanson Road.[23]

Bluff Creek

The world at large met Bigfoot in 1958, when a construction team led by Ray Wallace began expanding Highway 96 near Bluff Creek, north of tiny Weitchpec, in Humboldt County. Beginning in August, Jerry Crew—the party's bulldozer driver—reported finding many 16-inch humanoid footprints around the work site, separated by an average 4-foot stride. Crew made plaster casts of the tracks, and journalists trumpeted the story of "Bigfoot" in newspapers nationwide, luring Canadian researcher John Green and others to Bluff Creek.[24]

Fresh tracks continued to appear around Bluff Creek through 1958 and into 1959, apparently produced by at least two different sets of feet. Eyewitness sightings were also reported. Ray Wallace was involved in many of the sightings and reports, a circumstance that had unfortunate results four decades later.[25]

Wallace died at age 84, on November 26, 2002. Ten days later, a rash of media stories appeared, claiming that Wallace "invented the legend of Bigfoot" in 1958. Relatives declared that Wallace and

New 'Sasquatch' found

—it's called Bigfoot

The press hails Bigfoot's appearance at Bluff Creek in 1958. *Courtesy of Michael Newton*

his brother Wilbur had used wooden feet to produce Bigfoot tracks, not only around Bluff Creek, but throughout the Pacific Northwest. Son Michael told reporters, "Ray L. Wallace was Bigfoot. In reality, Bigfoot just died."[26]

Clearly, Wallace *did not* "invent" Bigfoot, since aboriginal stories of the huge bipeds predate arrival of the first white settlers in North America, and the first report from Spanish California dates from 1769, 149 years before Wallace was born. Wallace did fake *some* footprints with crudely-carved wooden blocks; he also tried to profit from his hoaxes by offering nonexistent Bigfoot films—and live captive specimens—for sale to the highest bidder from 1967 through 1979. John Green and other serious researchers recognized him as a fraud and never took him seriously. Only in death did Wallace receive the undeserved recognition he craved—including belated promotion on *CBS Evening News* by Dan Rather, in January 2003.[27]

The 1960s

The Sasquatch "flap" around Bluff Creek in 1958-59 produced more sightings in the 1960s, with at least 84 specific reports on file for the decade. Self-styled "skeptics" insist that Bluff Creek publicity encouraged hoaxers to claim their share of the spotlight. Open-minded researchers suggest that worldwide media coverage simply encouraged witnesses to share their stories without fear of crushing ridicule.

Geographically, Bigfoot sightings in the 1960s emerged from 22 of California's 58 counties. Fourteen northern counties produced 65 sightings: 18 from Humboldt County; 13 from Trinity; 8 from Siskiyou; 5 from Tuolumne; 4 each from Del Norte and Mendocino; 3 each from Butte and Plumas; 2 each from Alameda and Calaveras; one each from Marin, Sutter and Tehama. A 66th report is vaguely placed in "northern California."[28]

Sightings from central California in the Sixties include five reports from three counties: three from Mariposa, with one each from Fresno and Madera. In southern California, outside Bigfoot's "normal" range, four counties contributed 13 cases: six from San Diego, four from San Bernardino, plus one each from Los Angeles, Santa Barbara and Ventura.[29]

Mono County, on the Nevada border, produced the first of two sightings in 1960. On August 4, two sisters at East Lake saw a biped "larger than human," covered in "black or dark red" hair. Later that year, a five-year-old witness reported a tall green-eyed monster prowling outside his home near Lake Elsinore, in Riverside County.[30]

In mid-December 1961, eight-year-old Mike Clark camped with his father and five brothers near Bald Mountain, in Siskiyou County. While the boys cooked lunch, their fire was twice extinguished by large snowballs hurled from a nearby hillside. Suspecting their dad, the boys ran to catch him, but instead saw a "brown-colored man" who fled, leaving 19-inch tracks.[31]

The year 1962 produced two reports. In June, Mendocino County residents Robert Hatfield and Bud Jenkins claimed that Bigfoot left four-toed, 16-inch footprints around their home, near Fort Bragg. The prowler also marked one wall with an 11-inch handprint. Two months later, motorist Joseph Wattenbarger saw an 8-foot primate covered with "dirty silver" hair in Siskiyou County.[32]

Reports multiplied in 1963, with five on file. The most unusual, by far, was an unnamed hunter's claim that a white-haired Sasquatch carried him back to camp after the hunter suffered injuries in a fall. A less friendly creature frightened a guard at Vandenberg Air Force Base, in Santa Barbara County. Pilots Alden Hoover and Lennart

Bigfoot's California domain. Courtesy of US Geological Survey

Strand snapped aerial photos of something "half-bear, half-gorilla" near Sonora, on February 28. Screams alone marked Bigfoot's August visit to Big Bear City, while a deputy sheriff found hundreds of 15-inch tracks with a 5-foot stride at Leland Meadow (Tuolumne County) in December.[33]

Five reports emerged in 1964, none with specific dates. In July, campers on Mt. Tamalpais were disturbed by two primates "chittering" to one another in the woods. They only saw one of the beasts, estimating its weight at 200 pounds. That same summer, a father and son dodged rocks hurled by a shaggy biped near Escondido, in San Diego County. Near Jamul, in the same county, a foul-smelling "juvenile" Sasquatch killed three cows on the MGM Ranch, leaving humanoid footprints behind. Autumn produced Herb Brown's sighting of a Bigfoot chasing deer outside La Porte (Kings County), and November found a hairy "animal-man" prowling around an abandoned dairy near Fillmore (Ventura County).[34]

John Green provides the only case from 1965. That summer, Jan and Jim Gorell were camped in the San Gorgonio Mountains (San Bernardino County) when a "big black mass" with glowing eyes loomed out of the darkness beyond their campfire. It was hairy, with long arms, no visible neck, and stood 9-10 feet tall.[35]

Six reports were logged in 1966, all involving aggressive primates. Bob Kelley shot at a Sasquatch that peered through his cabin windows near Wildwood, in January.

In April, five campers near Weaverville watched Bigfoot prowl through their campsite, hurling trash containers about. Near San Diego, in July, a tall reddish-colored primate ransacked a car while five picnickers watched. That same month, at Fontana in San Bernardino County, Bigfoot scratched a boy and tore his clothes. On August 27, still in Fontana, a mud-covered biped that smelled "like a dead animal" rushed Jerri Mendenhall's car and snatched at her through an open window. Around the same time, at Albion Flat in Mendocino County, two "very large and hairy animals" killed several sheep in full view of two witnesses.[36]

The sole report from 1967 ranks as one of the most important incidents—or greatest hoaxes—in the history of cryptozoology. That case, and the startling film it produced, are fully described in Chapter 7.

We have seven cases from 1968, the first involving another airborne sighting by two pilots. Robert James Jr. and Leroy Larwick were flying over Confidence Ridge, near Yosemite National Park, on January 6, when they saw an apelike creature 10-12 feet tall. Larwick snapped a photo (which remains unpublished), then landed to photograph the creature's 20-inch footprints. Larry Weaver saw Bigfoot fording a river near Weaverville on April 6, then complained that a female specimen chased him for 30 minutes the following day. On April 8, in the same neighborhood, Mike Melton saw a Sasquatch drinking from a stream. Early July brought a sighting of a 4.5-foot "baby Bigfoot" from Bullfrog Lake in Tulare County. Days later, on July 11, campers saw Bigfoot pass their camp near Salyer, in Trinity County. In November, a squad of Marines met a hairy biped while on night maneuvers at Camp Pendleton, near San Diego.[37]

The decade ended with violence. In June, Bob Kelley and his family watched Bigfoot brawl with dogs at the Wildwood Inn, in the Shasta-Trinity National Forest. An 8-foot female specimen watched Charles and Kevin Jackson burning trash at Oroville on July 12, while a pair of primates took food from a Maple Spring resident's porch in late summer. In November, Mike Scott fired shots at a Sasquatch in Calaveras Big Trees State Park, but the creature escaped.[38]

Two other cases from the Sixties are undated, but deserve mention here. One involves a forestry worker who claims that Bigfoot followed him along the road from Willits to Fort Bragg. The other comes from witness "Scott M." and six companions, who claim an encounter with "Little Foot" near Strawberry, in Tuolumne County. They saw nothing, but heard "elfin-like voices" outside their cabin, reporting that "the voices were numerous and came, then went, as if marching in a line." A snowfall covered any tracks that might have existed.[39]

The 1970s

This decade produced 169 specific claims of Bigfoot encounters, plus published claims of "several" or "frequent" sightings in certain regions which included no specifics. For the first time, southern California dominated the field, with 36 detailed sightings from Los Angeles County alone. Other counties with multiple sightings included Humboldt, Shasta and Trinity (11 each); Mendocino (9); Tuolumne (8); San Bernardino (7); Kern and Siskiyou (6 each); Del Norte, Plumas and San Diego (5 each); El Dorado, Riverside and Tehama (4 each); Calaveras and Inyo (3 each); Alpine, Fresno, Mariposa, Modoc, Mono and Tulare (2 each). Single sightings were logged from Butte, Lake, Madera, Merced, Monterey, Nevada, Placer, Santa Barbara, Sonoma and Tulare Counties. Additionally, Four cases were vaguely reported from "northern" and "central" California; "frequent" sightings were claimed for the Sierra Nevada Mountains; and six reports cited place names such as Round Mountain, which occur in multiple counties.[40]

While witnesses in 20 cases from the 1970s could not recall specific dates—or even years—for their Bigfoot encounters, those with dates attached break down chronologically as follows: 12 each in 1970 and 1971, 13 in 1972, 20 in 1973, 17 in 1974, 13 each in 1975 and 1976, 23 in 1977, 16 in 1978, and 10 in 1979.[41] While space precludes detailed examination of each incident, we can establish certain trends.

Fifty-one of the decade's cases involve phenomena attributed to Bigfoot, but present no actual sightings. Of those, 26 involved unexplained noises, 13 reported discovery of oversized humanoid footprints, and one involved a foul odor of unknown origin. Three cases combined tracks and sounds, one coupled sounds with a smell "like sulphur or something rotting," and one placed 21-inch tracks near the spot where a steer was found wedged in the crotch of a tree with its neck broken. One hunter reported a "feeling or being watched," and two truckers asleep in their rig woke in darkness when some unseen prowler shook the vehicle. Hikers found an "A-frame type of nest" in one case, another found unidentified hair snagged on a tree, and two witnesses collected feces which was analyzed and "could not be traced to bear or primate, but had a very diverse diet."[42]

While fear is common among Bigfoot witnesses, few claim acts of aggression. In terms of predation, one 1970s report describes two apelike creatures stealing sacks of grain at Albion (Mendocino County), while two place Bigfoot or its tracks in the proximity of slaughtered deer, and another links large footprints to the death of a steer found in a tree. One hearsay report from "J.B." claims that Bigfoot disarmed a Marine on guard duty at Twentynine Palms and bent his rifle "almost in two." Forester Jaime Guzman also asserts that Bigfoot chased him to his pickup truck, near Rice Creek in Plumas County, whereupon Guzman lost consciousness. Researcher Ray Crowe reports that Guzman "can't seem to explain his blacking out in the truck, except maybe from having seen something that scared him so bad."[43]

The decade's two reports of human fatalities are inconclusive, to say the least. The first supposed victim, trucker Bob Foreacre, reportedly vanished near San Diego in 1970, while searching for Bigfoot tracks with companion Jackson Moore, but the case remains unsolved. Prior to his death in 2000, Rich Grumley, former director of the California Bigfoot Organization, claimed knowledge of a case from the "mid-to-late 1970s," wherein Bigfoot attacked campers near Bishop (Inyo County) and "killed several people." The report came third-hand from a former Bishop policeman, via attorney "Matt M.," and is not supported by official documents.[44]

Modern reports of Bigfoots slain or wounded by humans are equally infrequent. Witness "Allen" relays the tale of a Madera County hunter who saw a Sasquatch flattened by an eighteen-wheeler but "would deny it to his grave for fear of ridicule." John Green also reports that two girls found a dead and decomposed Bigfoot near Happy Camp (Siskiyou County) in June 1971. As usual, the corpse was not preserved. A third report, from Lyle Vann, describes a severed Sasquatch foot found in a bear trap and later shown to Vann by an unnamed trichologist (hair expert) in her "hidden office" at UCLA.[45]

Most witnesses describe Bigfoot as a bipedal primate standing six to eight feet tall, covered with hair that ranges in color from black to pure white, with shades of brown and red between the two extremes. Specimens as short as three and four feet are described in some reports, while veritable giants appear in others. Nine- and ten-foot primates are not uncommon, and the Bigfoot seen at Palmdale on December 27, 1975 was "about twice as tall as a man." The largest specimen on record stood 17 feet tall (as measured from an overhanging limb), had a chest 8-10 feet wide, and stood on legs that "were bigger around than [the witness's] pudgy little body." Perhaps the strangest case, reported by Adele Childress from Saugus, involved a Sasquatch seen in October 1974, wearing "a glowing, blue belt around its waist.[46]

Multiple-witness sightings of Bigfoot are fairly common, but meetings with multiple creatures are rare indeed. Witness "M.S." saw two "dark hairy creatures," one taller than the other, at his family's Shasta County camp, one night in August 1970. They seemed to be "negotiating" the retrieval of a food bag hanging from a tree, 15 feet off the ground. The other case, reported to researcher Matt Moneymaker by Sgt. Doug Huse of the San Diego County Sheriff's Department, involves a family of "Zoobies" seen sometime between December 1971 and February 1972. The witness, a "Dr. Baddour," claimed to have seen three creatures together: a 7-foot "father," a 5-foot "mother," and a presumed juvenile 3-4 feet tall.[47]

The 1980s

The 1980s offer 109 Bigfoot reports from 32 California counties. Sightings were more evenly distributed than in the 1970s, with 9 each from Humboldt and Los Angeles Counties; 7 from Del Norte; 5 each from Butte, Kern, Shasta, Siskiyou, Sonoma and Tulare; 4 each from El Dorado, Lassen, Mendocino, Riverside, San Diego and Trinity; 3 each from Fresno, Inyo, Nevada, Plumas, San Bernardino and Tuolumne; 2 each from Alpine, Modoc and Ventura; plus single sightings from Calaveras, Madera, Marin, Mono, Monterey, Napa, Santa Cruz and Sierra.[48]

Chronologically, the sightings broke down as follows: 13 each in 1980 and 1981; 9 in 1982; 5 in 1983; 6 in 1984; 12 each in 1985 and 1986; 8 in 1987; 15 in 1988; and 9 in 1989. Eight other sightings were recorded from the decade without reference to specific years.[49]

In 46 alleged Bigfoot encounters from the 1980s, no primates were seen. Twenty-five cases involved strange sounds attributed to Sasquatch, six were limited to rank odors, and six involved discovery of oversized footprints. Seven more cases mixed sounds with footprints, smells, or stone-throwing. Two final incidents involved a claim of hunting dogs frightened by some unseen creature, and a hiker who "felt" he was being observed.[50]

No reports of violent Bigfoot aggression emerged from the 1980s, though several witnesses reported stone-throwing by some unseen forest prankster. Evidence of Bigfoot's omnivorous appetite comes from sightings of a creature taking garbage from a Sonoma County dump, catching fish from a stream in Del Norte County, and stealing a deer hunter's kill in Shasta County. Witness Sherry Lancaster reportedly photographed a Tulare County specimen, sometime in the early 1980s, but her photo has not been published.[51]

A unique Bigfoot sighting came from Santa Catalina Island in October 1987. Witness Peter Hameline offered no explanation for the creature's appearance, 22 miles offshore from Los Angeles, but

Sightings of Bigfoot "families" still persist.
Courtesy of William Rebsamen

Wm Rebsamen
© 2003

he assured researcher Bobbie Short that "I would never, ever hoax." Hameline was camped with his brother's family on the night in question, but only he saw the six-foot-tall biped covered with reddish-brown hair. No other reports place Bigfoot on the island.[52]

The 1990s

The last decade of the twentieth century produced 252 specific reports of Bigfoot encounters statewide. Del Norte County led the pack with 35 reports; Humboldt logged 26; Trinity produced 22; Plumas and Siskiyou claimed 17 each; Shasta filed 12; San Luis Obispo reported 11; Butte and San Bernardino logged 10 each; Fresno, Los Angeles and Tuolumne claimed 9 each; Lassen and Santa Cruz reported 7 each; Mendocino logged 6; El Dorado, Kern, Mariposa and Modoc each filed 4; Monterey logged 3; Inyo, Madera and Tulare each produced 2; while single sightings came from Alpine, Calaveras, Glenn, Imperial, Merced, Mono, Nevada, Orange, Placer, Riverside, San Diego, San Mateo, Quincy, Sierra, Sonoma and Tehama. Five sightings from "northern" and "central" California specified no clear location.[53]

Forty-one percent of the 1990s reports—104 in all—include no actual sightings of Bigfoot. The largest number, 41, refer to unexplained sounds, including one claim of "communications heard between two separate animals," and two reports of unseen creatures gibbering in "backwards English." Another 23 cases involve large footprints, while three refer to unidentified smells. Twenty-six reports combine tracks, sounds or smells with other incidents: discovery of unknown hair, stone-throwing, feces, and animals frightened or slain. Eleven incidents include none of the usual signs, but blame Bigfoot for stacking rocks, snatching dogs, breaking trees, and so forth.[54]

The 1990s produced 11 claims of encounters with multiple unknown primates. One report offered no sighting, only "vocal communications between two separate animals," but the rest include direct observations. Five cases involve sightings of two creatures of roughly equal size; two of those cases included humanoid footprints, one measuring 21 inches. Three reports claim sightings of Bigfoot families: one involved a large adult with two smaller specimens; one featured two adults with a hairless infant; and the last involved a 15-foot male, strolling with an 11-foot female and 4-foot presumed offspring. A Butte County witness saw four bipeds walking in single file, each carrying a "huge bone" that was "bleached," with no flesh remaining. Researcher Ray Crowe notes that "the bones were so large and long, [the] witness could not imagine their source." Finally, two men in Del Norte County hold the world record for an unknown primate sighting, claiming that they saw 15 apelike creatures fishing for salmon along the Smith River. The band's shaggy leader carried something that "looked like a big stick or spear."[55]

Unknown California primates of the Nineties were often surprising in appearance and behavior, aside from their numbers. One of the largest on record—a 20-foot "tree nymph," further described as "a man made of bark"—was allegedly seen in Madera County, during August 1995. Two bipeds seen by a Lassen County witness supposedly wore "loin cloths," while two Plumas County callers warned police of a "black figure" in "dark clothing," crossing a rural highway. In November 1997, four tourists saw an 8-foot creature attack sea lions on a Mendocino County beach, suffering bites on one leg for its trouble.[56]

Nor were animals alone in being victimized by Bigfoot. The 1990s produced nine supposed cases of Sasquatch aggression toward humans, but several are vague. One involved an "intimidation approach," wherein Bigfoot pounded its fist on the ground and approached a hiker. Two other creatures reportedly shook vehicles, while three hurled stones at witnesses. In 1992, a Butte County resident claimed that Bigfoot followed him home to his cabin, peered through windows, and struck the outer walls. Three years later, witnesses at some undisclosed location reported a Sasquatch chasing their car and blamed the beast for disemboweling a dog. The most unusual (and least credible) case involved a May 1997 claim that Bigfoot had attacked "a bunch of Mexican loggers" in Mendocino County, leaving several with broken bones. That case was "researched" by hoaxer Ray Wallace, and should likely be rejected for that reason alone.[57]

Remarkably, the 1990s also produced four alleged photos or films of Bigfoot, though all remain unpublished. The first is a 29-second film shot by researcher Scott Herriott near the Klamath River, in October 1992. It purports to show a "grayish ape-like thing with pointed head and red glowing eyes." Two years later, a pair of youths reportedly photographed an 8-foot creature that left 17-inch footprints near Bishop. In August 1995, an L.A.-based television crew, including a *Playmate* model, supposedly caught Bigfoot on tape near Crescent City, in Del Norte County. The model later discussed her experience on Jay Leno's TV program and on *Hard Copy*. Finally, in July 1998, photographed a Sasquatch near Big Bar, in Butte County.[58]

Do California hikers share the woods with giant unknown primates? *Courtesy of William Rebsamen*

Twenty-First-Century Cases

During 2000-08, California witnesses reported 183 alleged Bigfoot encounters. The decade started strong, with 43 reports in 2000 and 46 in 2001, then dropped to 20 in 2002, 26 in 2003, 13 in 2004, 19 in 2005, 10 in 2006, 7 in 2007, and 3 in 2008. Reports emerged from 30 counties: 22 each from El Dorado and Humboldt; 19 from Tuolumne; 12 from Butte; 11 from Shasta; 9 from Del Norte; 8 each from Siskiyou and Trinity; 7 from Mono; 6 from Tulare; 5 each from Alpine, Nevada and Placer; 4 each from Calaveras, Fresno, Los Angeles, Plumas and San Bernardino; 3 from and Santa Cruz; 2 each from Kern and Modoc; with single reports from Contra Costa, Mendocino, Monterey, Orange, San Diego, Sierra, Solano and Sonoma. One report from "northern California" specified no location.[59]

For the first time ever, claims of Bigfoot encounters based on circumstantial evidence outnumbered eyewitness sightings by a margin of 55 to 45 percent. A total of 54 "possible" cases involved reports of strange sounds alone. Another 25 involved discovery of large humanoid footprints, some of which were photographed or cast in plaster. Seventeen cases involved mixed evidence: sounds with smells, tracks and broken trees, stone-throwing accompanied by vocalizations, and so forth. Four cases involved vandalism, slaughter of poultry and thrown objects with no traditional signs of Bigfoot.[60]

At press time for this book, only two twenty-first-century witnesses had reported sightings of multiple primates. A Plumas County resident saw a man-sized creature with its "child" in May 2000, while a fisherman in El Dorado County saw two creatures—one 8.5 feet tall, the other 4-5 feet tall—in August 2005. Aside from incidents of rock- and log-tossing by unseen pranksters, no physical aggression has been claimed. Most of the creatures sighted conformed to typical descriptions, but one was an "albino," and another's face "glowed with a reddish hue." A group of campers in Siskiyou county allegedly videotaped a "distressed Bigfoot" in July 2000, but their tape has not been aired.[61]

Undated Reports

Finally, 78 California Bigfoot reports include no dates for the supposed events. Eight of those also omit any identifiable location. Of the remainder, 20 come from Humboldt County; 10 from Del Norte; 7 from Siskiyou; 6 from Los Angeles; 5 each from Shasta and Trinity;

3 from Butte; 2 from Mendocino; with single cases from Mariposa, Nevada, Orange, Placer, Plumas, San Bernardino, Sierra, Solano, Sonoma, Tahoma and Tulare.[62]

Twenty-three undated reports claim Bigfoot encounters without actual sightings. Five involve discovery of humanoid tracks (and one large muddy handprint), while two others involve only sounds. Eight include a mixed bag of evidence: tracks, sounds, and/or foul odors coupled with hair samples, stacked rocks, thrown objects, and discovery of dead animals. The last eight present features including broken or uprooted trees, mutilated animals, and the lifting of a parked car by some unidentified force.[63]

Eleven undated reports claim sightings of multiple apelike bipeds, but details suggest that several are garbled versions of some earlier account. The IBS cites two cases in which a female Sasquatch mimicked a mother's example by holding an infant aloft, and while those reports list different counties (Butte and Plumas), with different witnesses ("Carene" and "Rita"), both come from the same researcher. Likewise, the IBS assigns two case numbers to one incident, Jim Karl's sighting of two four-foot creatures seen in Del Norte County. The same happens with witness "Guy's" sighting of three primates near Eureka. Witness "J. Gibson" also saw three creatures together, at Castaic Lake in Los Angeles County. An unnamed Butte County woman saw two bipeds of different colors, while witness Jackson Moore allegedly filmed two primates foraging for food in Siskiyou County, then lost the film when they attacked him.[64]

Our undated reports include only one sighting of Bigfoot dressed in "tattered and torn" clothes, but multiple reports allege aggressive behavior, including several apparent homicides. Minor incidents include five incidents of rock- or log-throwing (resulting in one broken arm), one brief pursuit of a motorcycle, lifting a parked car, and striking a house with a fist. Three reports blame Bigfoot for snatching or mutilating animals. Typically exaggerated tales from hoaxer Ray Wallace claims Sasquatch abductions of Native American women and killings of three unnamed prospectors. Finally, Jackson Moore claims that his film of Bigfoot, accompanied by hair samples, was lost when two beasts attacked him and killed his unnamed partner.[65]

Skeptics note the lack of scientific proof supporting any of the Bigfoot sightings noted in this chapter, and without a specimen in hand for study, it is difficult—if not impossible—to prove Bigfoot's existence. On the other hand, there is a possibility that we already have the next best thing to a live specimen.

Some researchers believe that we have had it—and, for the most part, have stubbornly ignored it—for the better part of half a century.

Chapter 7

Patty

Washington resident Roger Patterson became fascinated with Bigfoot after reading an article by Ivan Sanderson, titled "The Strange Story of America's Abominable Snowman," in the December 1959 issue of *True* magazine. Patterson subsequently organized the Abominable Snowmen Club of America, operating from his home in Yakima, and in 1966 published a book on the subject, titled *Do Abominable Snowmen of America Really Exist?*[1]

The next logical step was to seek proof of Bigfoot's existence. Early in 1967, Patterson decided to launch his own search and document the journey on film, with an eye toward commercial release. During August and September he scoured the countryside around Mount St. Helens with companion Bob Gimlin, then Patterson's wife phoned with news that fresh tracks had surfaced near Bluff Creek, California. Patterson and Gimlin drove south on October 1 and set up camp, making daily forays on horseback.[2]

In preparation for the journey, Patterson had rented a Cine-Kodak K-100 16mm movie camera from Sheppard's Drive-In Camera Shop, in Yakima. On October 18, the shop's owner contacted police, reporting that his property was overdue. By that time, Patterson had shot 76 feet of film depicting forest landscapes, but he had not managed to locate a single Bigfoot track.[3]

On October 20 he found something even better.

Patty's Screen Test

Patterson and Gimlin left their camp at noon on October 20, 1967. Ninety minutes later, as they reconstructed the event in interviews, they met a female Sasquatch six to seven feet tall, weighing an estimated 350-400 pounds, walking along a sandbar 50 feet or so in front of them. Patterson's horse reared in alarm, while Gimlin's retreated. Their packhorse bolted in panic, forcing Gimlin to release its reins, in order to control his own mount.[4]

By that time, Patterson had either leaped or fallen to the ground, clutching his rented camera. He ran across rugged ground, parallel to the Bigfoot's course of travel, and began filming the creature from an estimated range of 80 feet. Gimlin dismounted, tracking the hairy biped with a rifle, while Patterson used up the final 24 feet of film on his camera's 100-foot roll.[5]

As the creature—later dubbed "Patty," after Patterson's surname—vanished into the forest, Gimlin prepared to follow on horseback. Patterson, now separated from his horse and rifle, called for Gimlin to wait while he reloaded the Kodak. Once that was done, they followed the Bigfoot's path for a considerable distance but never glimpsed it again. Only footprints remained, measuring 14.5 inches long by 6 inches wide.[6]

Racing back to camp, Patterson and Gimlin retrieved bags of plaster, then returned to the site of their encounter and made casts of two footprints, one right and one left. Noting the depth of the tracks, Patterson also performed an experiment—filmed by Gimlin—in which he stood atop a tree stump and jumped off to make his own footprints. In no case, even with the extra height and force, did his tracks match the depth of Patty's. When it began to rain at 5:30 a.m. on October 21. Gimlin and Patterson went back again, preserving the tracks as best they could by covering them with tree bark.[7]

Between his second and third visits to the sandbar, Patterson kept busy spreading word of his encounter with Bigfoot. He drove first to Al Hodgson's store in Willow Creek, but found it closed at 6:00 p.m. on October 20. He then phoned Hodgson at home, and they met at the store with other locals, where Patterson described the adventure. At 9:30 p.m. he phoned a reporter for the Eureka *Times-Standard,* which headlined the story on October 21.[8]

Al Hodgson, meanwhile, called Don Abbott, curator of anthropology at the Royal British Columbia Museum, asking him to contact Canadian Bigfoot researcher John Green and inquire about availability of tracking dogs. Green, in turn, phoned colleague René

A still frame from the Patterson film. *Courtesy of Michael Newton*

Casts of giant tracks made after the Patterson-Gimlin sighting. *Courtesy of Michael Newton*

Dahinden (1930-2001) in San Francisco and arranged to meet him at Bluff Creek. Both men arrived by noon on October 21, but they missed Patterson and Gimlin. The two monster-hunters had left for Yakima at 4:00 a.m., bearing their precious film.[9]

Aftermath

Patterson delivered the film to his brother-in-law, Al DeAtley, for developing on October 21. The film required processing under the patented Kodak K-12 system, restricted to specific licensed laboratories in large cities, but DeAtley later claimed that he could not remember where he took the film, and Patterson refused to identify the lab, saying, "I had them done at a private place. It would jeopardize the man's job if it were told." Sadly, he took the secret to his grave in 1972 and thus added another layer of controversy to the already-sensational incident.[10]

In any case, the film had been processed by October 22, when John Green visited DeAtley's home. Patterson arrived soon thereafter, and DeAtley took him to the basement for a private screening before Green viewed the film. René Dahinden turned up around 3:00 p.m. with Bigfoot researcher Jim McClarin, and all five men watched the film again before discussing the best course of future action. Dahinden and Green finally convinced Patterson that scientists in British Columbia might be more receptive to his evidence than any in the United States.[11]

Meanwhile, taxidermist, tracker, and Bigfoot researcher Robert Titmus (1919-97) made his way to Bluff Creek for a personal investigation of the Patterson-Gimlin sighting. Titmus was himself a Bigfoot witness and had systematically pursued evidence of the creature's existence since 1958. He found the tracks preserved by Patterson and many more besides, following them to a point in the woods where Patty had "sat down for some time among the ferns," apparently watching Patterson and Gimlin from a distance of 125-150 yards. Titmus made several plaster casts of tracks which, unlike the prints created by carved model feet, "show a vast difference in each imprint, such as toe placement, toe gripping force, pressure ridges and breaks, weight shifts, weight distribution, depth, etc."[12]

In short, he went home convinced that Patty was real.

Analyzing the Film

On October 26, 1967, Dr. Ian McTaggart-Cowan from the University of British Columbia hosted two screenings of Patterson's film in Vancouver. The first audience included scientists from the Royal British Columbia Museum and private researchers, among them Patterson and Gimlin, John Green, René Dahinden, Bob Titmus and publisher David Hancock. The second viewing, at Vancouver's Georgia Hotel, was the first public airing for journalists.[13]

While no formal transcript of the first viewing exists, John Green noted that scientists in the audience raised three objections to the film's authenticity. First, they claimed that while Patty had obvious female breasts, she "walked like a man." Second, they protested that no female specimens of higher primates have hairy breasts. And finally, they observed Patty's sagital crest, which they claimed is only found in male gorillas.[14]

Dr. Grover Krantz (1931-2002), professor of physical anthropology at Washington State University and a staunch Bigfoot believer, noted that none of those asked for opinions concerning Patterson's film in October 1967 was a primatologist. He went on to observe that human females "generally walk rather differently from males, but there is no such contrast in apes." Krantz also dismissed the complaint about hairy breasts among apes, deeming the coat of hair in a temperate climate "perfectly reasonable." Finally, Krantz observed that "a sagital crest is not a male characteristic...; on the contrary it is a consequence of absolute size alone." Patty was larger than a normal male gorilla, prompting Krantz to state that "[a]ll of the creature's anatomical and functional traits are fully consistent with its identification as a female."[15]

In November 1967 *Life* magazine proposed a feature article on the Patterson film, but before committing to the project, *Life*'s editors demanded a screening at New York's American Museum of Natural History. Patterson obliged, but later noted that the scientists assembled for the viewing settled for a single run-through of the footage, with no freeze-frames or measurements taken, then declared without explanation that the film was "not kosher." Patterson left that session convinced that the experts had prejudged the film before he arrived in New York.[16]

Life's management was swiftly losing interest, but they agreed to obtain a second opinion from Bronx Zoo curators, who viewed the film twice with several stop-frames. Despite seeming more open-minded at first, zoo officials claimed to find "something wrong" with the film, but declined to specify the problem. The *Life* story fell through.[17]

While in New York, Patterson contacted Ivan Sanderson, who in turn called editors of *Argosy* magazine. *Argosy* played the film for a quartet of scientists, plus an official from the U.S. Department of the Interior, an editor from *National Geographic,* and various local reporters. While *National Geographic* dismissed the film, and the *New York Times* ignored it completely, none of the other viewers proclaimed it a hoax. Sanderson's resultant article, published by *Argosy* in February 1968, alluded to separate screenings for unnamed Hollywood special-effects experts, who allegedly pronounced themselves unable to duplicate Patty on film.[18]

John Green took a copy of Patterson's film to Hollywood in 1969, and found experts willing to defend Patty on-record. Ken Peterson, a senior executive for Disney Studios, told Green that his staff could not duplicate Patterson's film without using animated footage, since their cutting-edge animatronics were inadequate to emulate Patty's movements. If the film was hoaxed, Peterson opined, then Patty must be a man in an ape suit.[19]

With that thought in mind, Green consulted Janos Prohaska (1919-74), Hollywood's reigning creature-costume designer, whose credits included *Land of the Giants, Lost in Space, The Outer Limits,* and *Star Trek.* After viewing Patterson's film, Prohaska said, "You could see all the muscles in the body....It didn't move like a costume at all. It looked to me very, *very* real. If that was a costume, that was *the* best I have ever seen."[20]

Patterson's film received a warmer reception in Russia, where government-sponsored research into unknown primates dates from the 1920s. Dr. Dmitri Donskoy, chairman of the Biomechanics Department at Moscow's Central Institute of Physical Culture, declared in 1973 that Patty's movements on-screen revealed "a fully spontaneous and highly efficient pattern of locomotion...with all the particular movements combined in an integral whole that presents a smoothly operating and coherent system." In short, he concluded, "a walk as demonstrated by the creature in the film is absolutely non-typical of man."[21]

A quarter-century later, in 1997, Russian hominologists Dmitri Bayanov and Igor Bourtsev proclaimed that Patterson's film "has passed all our tests and scrutinies. This gives us ground to ask: Who other than God or natural selection is sufficiently conversant with anatomy and biomechanics to 'design' a body which is so perfectly harmonious in terms of structure and function?"[22]

Finally, judgment of Patty comes down to the film-speed of Patterson's rented camera. The Cine-Kodak K-100 had a variable dial, permitting film to be exposed at speeds of 16, 24, 32, 48, or 64 frames per second—and, in fact, could also be set for intermediate speeds between those marked choices. Patterson captured Patty on 952 frames of film, but he neglected to note the setting.[23]

The film's speed is critical in judging Patty's gait, and claims that the movie depicts a man in an ape suit. Dr. D.W. Grieve, an anatomist and reader in biomechanics at London's Royal Free Hospital School of Medicine, studied the film extensively and issued the following judgment:

> "It is likely that the filming was done at either 16, 18 or 24 frames per second....If 16 fps is assumed, the cycle time and the time of swing [by arms and legs] are in a typical human combination but much longer in duration than one would expect from the stride and the pattern of limb movement. It is as if a human were executing a high speed pattern in slow motion....Similar conclusions apply to the combination of variables if we assume 18 fps....If the film was taken at 24 fps, Sasquatch walked with a gait pattern very similar in most respects to a man walking at high speed....The possibility of fakery is ruled out if the speed of the film was 16 or 18 fps."[24]

Must the mystery remain forever unsolved? Grover Krantz believed that Patterson's film speed could be calculated from his known height and length of his stride, plus his distance from Patty. A subject filmed at 24 feet per second would stand only three feet eight inches tall, while at 16 feet per second the height would be eight feet six inches. He concluded, "We may safely rule out 16 frames per second and accept the speed of 18 frames."[25]

Krantz also used four known measurements from the film site to calculate Patty's size. Specifically, the subject's stride averaged 81.5 inches, its footprints were 14.5 inches long and 4.5 inches wide at the heel, while the camera was 102 feet distant from Patty when the most famous frame of Patterson's film was exposed. Based on that data and a presumed film speed of 18 frames per second, Krantz calculated that Patty stood approximately 6 feet 6 inches tall, measured 28.2 inches across the shoulders, and weighed roughly 500 pounds.[26]

During 1994-97 the North American Science Institute, chaired by certified forensic examiner Jeff Glickman, performed a three-year computer analysis of Patterson's film, costing $100,000, and reached very different conclusions. The NASI's report estimated that Patty stood 7 feet 2 inches tall, with an 83-inch chest, 81.3-inch waist, and weighed 1,957 pounds. It's arms, at a calculated length of 43 inches, were "virtually beyond human standards, possibly occurring in one out of 52.5 million people." Patty's 40-inch legs were deemed "unusual by human standards, possibly occurring in one out of 1,000 people." Finally, "Nothing was found indicating the creature was a man in a costume (i.e., no seam or interfaces)."[27]

Hoax? Which Hoax?

It comes as no surprise that some viewers of the Patterson film—and others who have never bothered to watch it—regard the film as a hoax. However, the number of mutually exclusive "true solutions" proposed is rather astounding. At last count, no less than seven authors have "exposed" the hoax—including one who advanced two different suspects as "the man in the ape suit"!

Bigfoot hoaxes are a standard tabloid joke. *Courtesy of Michael Newton*

While various critics had long proclaimed that the Patterson film "must be fake" because "Bigfoot doesn't exist," the first detailed claim of a hoax surfaced in 1991, when researcher Peter Gutilla interviewed Clyde Reinke, a private investigator living in tiny Beatty, Nevada (population 1,154 in 2000). Reinke claimed responsibility for the Patterson film, as a former executive of American National Enterprises (ANE), a film company that produced eight motion pictures and distributed 20 more between 1966 and 1986. Reinke told Gutilla that Roger Patterson was "on the [ANE] payroll" in 1967, and that Reinke personally "signed Patterson's checks." Reinke named the "man in the suit" as one Jerry Romney, ANE's former insurance agent, who categorically denied any link to the film. Loren Coleman explains the story by claiming that ANE purchased Patterson's footage for use in a documentary titled *Bigfoot: Man or Beast?* but problems persist. Coleman dates that film from 1971, while the Internet Movie Database pegs it as a 1972 release—and does not list it among ANE's 22 recognized films. According to the research staff at Turner Classic Movies, *Bigfoot: Man or Beast?* was actually produced by Gemini-American Productions and distributed by Ellman Enterprises, neither with any apparent link to ANE.[28]

The next significant hoax claim surfaced in summer 1996. Mark Chorvinsky (1954-2005), a stage magician and editor/publisher of *Strange Magazine*, broke the story with a claim that "for years it has been 'generally known' in the Hollywood special effects makeup community that Academy Award winning makeup artist John Chambers fabricated the suit in the Patterson Bigfoot film." Chorvinsky first heard the rumor in 1992, later "confirming" it in interviews with Hollywood makeup artists Dave Kindlon and Rick Baker, both of whom got the story from unnamed third parties (but never from Chambers himself).[29]

While *Strange Magazine* had a limited readership, London's *Sunday Telegraph* reaches millions. On October 19, 1997—timed to correspond with the thirtieth anniversary of Patty's screen test—that paper ran a story headlined "Hollywood Admits to Bigfoot Hoax." The story read, in part:

> A piece of film, which for thirty years has been regarded as the most compelling evidence for the existence of Bigfoot...is a hoax, according to new claims. John Chambers, the man behind the *Planet of the Apes* films and the elder statesman of Hollywood's "monster makers," has been named by a group of Hollywood makeup artists as the person who faked Bigfoot. In an interview with Scott Essman, an American journalist, the veteran Hollywood director John Landis revealed "a makeup secret only six people know." Mr. Landis said: "That famous piece of film of Bigfoot walking in the woods that was touted as the real thing was just a suit made by John Chambers." He said he learned the information while working alongside Mr. Chambers on *Beneath the Planet of the Apes* in 1970.... Howard Berger, of Hollywood's KNB Effects Group, said it was common knowledge within the film industry that Mr. Chambers was responsible for a hoax that turned Bigfoot into a worldwide cult. Mike McCracken Jr., a makeup artist and associate of Mr. Chambers, said: "I'd say with absolute certainty that John was responsible."[30]

In fact, as Loren Coleman notes, Scott Essman was a friend of Mark Chorvinsky, promoting Chorvinsky's hoax tale from 1996.[31] It was thus neither "new," nor restricted to "only six people" in Hollywood. And while the claim may have been "common knowledge" to some, John Chambers himself was not among them.

A week after the story broke in London, on October 26, veteran Bigfoot researcher Roberta "Bobbie" Short traced Chambers to a California rest home and interviewed him there. Still lucid at age 74, Chambers denied any part in creating the Patterson film. He told Short that he "was good, but not that good," admittedly lacking the skill and/or materials required to fabricate such a lifelike suit in 1967. Chambers persisted in denial of the hoax reports until his death, on August 25, 2001.[32]

In fact, as any student of Hollywood special effects can confirm, the ape costumes that won Chambers an honorary Oscar for *Planet of the Apes* in 1969—and which appeared in its various sequels during 1970-73—consisted of rubber masks, gloves and feet, while the actors' bodies were concealed by normal clothing. No full-body ape suits were used, and folds in the material of other costumes filmed before the late-1970s advent of computer-generated imagery betrayed disguised actors to any discerning eye.

In short, there was no Chambers hoax.

Fourteen months after the *Sunday Telegraph*'s misguided expose, on December 28, 1998, Fox Television aired a documentary titled *World's Greatest Hoaxes: Secrets Revealed*. Part of the program focused on Bigfoot, with professional "skeptic" Kal Korff declaring Patterson's film a fake based on a "dark line" along Patty's spine. Korff also repeated the Reinke tale from 1991, naming Jerry Romney (despite his ongoing denials) as Patterson's "man in the suit." John Green fired back from Canada, declaring, "There is certainly a hoax involved here, but not the one claimed by Fox. They are the ones who were hoaxed."[33]

Two weeks after the Fox program aired, on January 11, 1999, *USA Today* and other American newspapers ran yet another "final solution" to the Patty problem. This time, the source was Cliff Crook, operator of the Bigfoot Central website based in Bothell, Washington. Crook claimed to see a metal "belt buckle" dangling from Patty in one frame of Patterson's film, saying, "When the guy in the suit turned to look at the camera, it probably snapped loose and dangled from the fur. It's a hoax. Why would Bigfoot be wearing a belt buckle?"[34]

Why, indeed?

The problem with Crook's theory is that, so far, no other researcher seems able to spot the offending "belt buckle." Christopher Murphy, cited in the 1999 press release as supporting Crook's theory, published a book *defending* Patterson's film in 2005—and omitted all mention of Crook from his text. Meanwhile, the Bigfoot Field Researchers Organization brands Crook himself as a serial photo-hoaxer. Upon release of his latest alleged Bigfoot snapshot in 2008, the BFRO proclaimed: "Mr. Crook has been serving up and attempting to market fake Bigfoot photos and other fabricated Bigfoot evidence for several years now and is well known for doing so among veterans in the Bigfoot research community. He claims to have been researching Bigfoot for 'longer than anyone.' This is far from the truth, and typical of the mistruths continually pumped out by this individual."[35]

Eighteen days after Cliff Crook's announcement, attorney Barry Woodard of Zillah, Washington, told the *Yakima Herald-Republic* that an unnamed client "approached him a few months ago after a network news program called questioning authenticity of the 1967 film." According to Woodard, the 58-year-old Washingtonian sought help in "negotiating a deal for rights to his story...as well as to explore any legal issues he might face as a result of his involvement in the hoax."[36] Another five years would elapse before the man of mystery was finally identified.

When veteran Sasquatch hoaxer Ray Wallace died on November 26, 2002, son Michael Wallace told the *Seattle Times* (and anyone else who would listen), "Ray L. Wallace was Bigfoot. The reality is, Bigfoot just died." Most mainstream media outlets accepted that claim at face value, failing to ask how Wallace, born in 1918, could have spawned Bigfoot stories predating the arrival of America's first white settlers—and some went even further. While Michael Wallace specifically denied any link between his father and the Patterson film, anthropologist David Daegling alleged that Ray "had a degree of involvement" in the filming, and Mark Chorvinsky jumped on the bandwagon, saying, "Ray told me that the Patterson film was a hoax, and he knew who was in the suit." Chorvinsky also claimed that Wallace "told Patterson where to go" for a probable Bigfoot sighting, and suggested that Ray's wife Elna wore the supposed ape costume.[37]

It goes without saying—or should, by this time—that nothing supports the claims made by Daegling, Chorvinsky, or anyone else linking Wallace and clan to the Patterson film.

Next in line to deride Patterson and his film was Greg Long, who claims a quarter-century of writing about Pacific Northwest mysteries. His first book, *Examining the Earthlight Theory* (1990), debunked UFO sightings around Yakima, Washington. His second, *The Making of Bigfoot* (2004), claims to expose "the real truth behind the Roger Patterson 'Bigfoot' film—a hoax that has managed to fool scores of scientists and millions of people around the world."[38]

Long sets the tone with a foreword by Kal Korff, who named Jerry Romney the Patty six years earlier, but who now supports Long's selection of a different actor. Writing from Prague, where he serves as president and CEO of something called "Critical Thinkers," Korff thundered: "Those who persist in being less than truthful about the now discredited and exposed Roger Patterson Bigfoot hoax film... should be ashamed of their dishonest behavior and finally admit the truth. The promoters should be condemned by the public and held accountable for their ongoing actions, if not investigated by the proper authorities for possible consumer fraud."[39]

Long echoed that arrogant tone in public and private comments, as when he told an audience assembled by the International Bigfoot Society, "The standards of evidence for the Bigfoot believers are extremely low. I have much higher standards, you know, like honesty and integrity."[40] It remains for Long's readers to judge that integrity.

More than eight years in the making, from autumn 1995 to March 2004, *The Making of Bigfoot* finally offers 466 pages of hearsay and speculation, unsupported by a single piece of solid evidence. Long's "real truth...revealed by basic science, critical thinking, and simple detective work" boils down to stories spun by two men who never met, and who contradict each other frequently.[41]

Long's first alleged witness is Washington resident Bob Heironimus, lawyer Barry Woodard's unnamed client from 1999 and the self-declared "man in the ape suit," who claims his story is supported by results of an undated, unreleased polygraph test. The other, Philip Morris, is a stage magician and costume-maker from North Carolina, who says he sold Roger Patterson a gorilla suit in 1967 but has no evidence to prove it.[42] Problems arise from comparison of statements by Heironimus and Morris, and from Long's attempts to reconcile the obvious discrepancies.

In his various statements to Long, Heironimus incorrectly placed the 1967 film at site *Willow* Creek, 20 miles southwest of *Bluff* Creek, but that glitch pales beside the problems created by his description of Patterson's ape suit. According to Heironimus, the suit he wore in 1967 consisted of three parts: a head, the legs, and "a corset or middle piece between the neck and waist." Heironimus said Patterson had personally skinned a "red horse," then glued fur from "an old fur coat" onto the hide, which "stunk" when he donned it. The legs felt like rubber hip boots and may have cinched at the waist with a drawstring, although Heironimus could not recall. The feet were "made of old house slippers that you used to see around," with five toes each and wrinkled cloth soles. The hands felt like stiff leather gloves, and the headpiece reminded Heironimus of "an old-time football helmet," with two inches of space between his face and its mask. Patty's breasts were "solid," rather than "bouncy," but Heironimus "never gave much thought" to how they were attached. After the filming, Patterson left the suit with Heironimus, whence it vanished forever to parts unknown.[43]

Philip Morris told Long a very different story in 2003. His one-size-fits-all gorilla suits were made of knitted cloth, with artificial fur composed of Dynel acrylic resin fibers, and came in *six* pieces, not three. Components included the head, a zipper-backed torso with arms and legs attached, two hands, and two feet. The feet (men's size 10-12) had neoprene rubber soles, not wrinkled cloth. The costume's molded rubber chest protruded "several inches" in front, with no option for feminine breasts.[44]

Clearly, the suits described by Heironimus and Morris bore no resemblance to each other. Still, Morris insisted that he sold one of his suits to Patterson in 1967, receiving payment in the form of a $335 postal money order which proved unverifiable. In an effort to resolve the contradictory descriptions, Morris claimed that Patterson had phoned him after receiving the suit, asking how to hide the 36-inch zipper, pad the shoulders, and extend the arms while "somebody else" prompted Patterson from the sidelines. Morris says he suggested a hairbrush, football shoulder pads, and sticks inside the sleeves that would somehow "screw onto" the gloves—a refinement that would have prevented Heironimus from donning the gloves as described in his tale. Patty's breasts baffled Morris, but Long surmised that "Patterson could have attached balloons filled with sand to the front of the suit."[45]

Despite insisting that Patterson had purchased and used one of his stock gorilla suits in 1967, Morris frankly admitted that Patty's film-face and the footprints cast at Bluff Creek bore no resemblance to the mask and feet sold with his costumes. Concerning the mask, Morris speculated that "Patterson could have replaced the nose on my mask with a prosthetic one"—though Heironimus made no such claim—or else replaced the stock mask with another model concocted via "emerging technology." Ignoring those discrepancies, Morris told Long, "When I saw the film on television, I knew within seconds that I was looking at my suit. I knew it! That suit was the style of my gorilla suit." He "proved" it with a photo of another ape suit, which Long describes as "the exact same type of gorilla suit Roger Patterson bought from Philip Morris." It bears no resemblance to Patty.[46]

Facing criticism from the day his book was published, Long replied in writing to a series of questions submitted by researcher Rich La Monica for publication on La Monica's Northeastern Ohio's Researchable Kryptids Accounts website. In that "interview," Long promised a "recreation of the 'Bigfoot' suit" employing "the exact same materials used by Philip Morris in 1967," plus "additional proof from me" supporting the Morris-Heironimus story.[47] As I write these words in December 2008, Long's promise remains unfulfilled.

A new take on Patterson's film emerged on November 26, 2006, when "Bigfoot researcher" M.K. Davis claimed that Patty was neither a Sasquatch nor a man in costume, but rather a "completely human" forest-dweller. Davis vowed that "everything on the film can be explained"—and would be, in a forthcoming documentary produced by one Pat Holbrook. In a subsequent taped interview with Tom Biscardi—himself linked to a "Bigfoot corpse" hoax in 2008—Davis contradicted himself, saying, "I never said that, that Bigfoot was human, I just said what was on the Patterson film was human....I don't even know if that's a Bigfoot or not, on that film. You know, maybe it is, maybe it isn't."[47] It comes as no surprise that Holbrook's documentary remains unseen—but Davis was not finished, yet.

The "Bluff Creek Massacre"

Perhaps frustrated by the cold reception to his first effort, M.K. Davis surfaced at Ohio's Salt Fork State Park in May 2008, for Don Keating's 20th Annual Ohio Bigfoot Conference. There, Davis advanced a "theory" that Patty was filmed several days prior to October 20, 1967, during the first of two Bluff Creek sojourns by Patterson and Gimlin. During their second visit, on October 20, Davis claims that Patterson, Gimlin, and "possibly others" were ambushed by a tribe of giant primates, all of which they shot in self-defense, then buried in a mass grave to avert prosecution for killing "nearly human" creatures. John Johnsen, founder of Grendel Films and Davis's apparent new partner, claimed that the tale was "verified" by unnamed individuals whom Davis interviewed, over a period of years.[49]

While that tale sparked heated controversy among Sasquatch researchers, veteran monster-hunter Joe Beelart added more fuel to the fire, suggesting that Bob Heironimus and/or Al DeAtley may have participated in the hypothetical slaughter. Long-winded speculation about grave sites and the hidden meaning of various cryptic remarks spanning 40-odd years stops far short of proving the massacre case.[50]

Last Words

Controversy still surrounds the Patterson film, growing more acrimonious (and more bizarre) as each new theory or solution surfaces. It is impossible to prove a negative, and the existence of Bigfoot cannot be documented scientifically without physical remains. That said, the following observations are uncontestable:

- First, it is impossible for *all* of the skeptics' solutions to be simultaneously true. If John Chambers made a costume for Patterson, Philip Morris is lying. If Morris made the suit, all of Mark Chorvinsky's Hollywood sources are wrong. No ape suit could accommodate Bob Heironimus, Jerry Romney, *and* Elna Wallace posing as Patty.

- Second, without hard evidence—the same standard demanded by outspoken skeptics—none of the speculation advanced by Chorvinsky, Clyde Reinke, Kal Korff, Greg Long, M.K. Davis, or anyone else proves anything whatsoever. Almost anything "may have happened," but proof of a hoax remains elusive.

- And finally, just as skeptics insist that no film or photograph can prove the existence of Bigfoot without supporting physical evidence, so debunking of Patterson's film cannot *disprove* the existence of unknown creatures in North America, or anywhere else on Earth. The shopworn argument that every film and photo must be fake because "such things do not exist" is simply false, and must hereafter be rejected for all time.

Chapter 8
Stranger Still

As if the creatures surveyed in preceding chapters are not strange enough, California also allegedly harbors more monsters, who fit none of the foregoing categories. Some appear to spring full-blown from ancient myths, while others resemble nothing known in folklore or science. Still, they are reported—or have been, within living memory—and they deserve inclusion here.

They Might Be Giants

Oversized humans appear in the legends of every culture. They populate fairy tales and surface regularly in low-budget horror films. Most skeptics, however, choose to ignore a substantial body of evidence suggesting that real-life giants once shared Earth with diminutive *Homo sapiens*.

The Miwok Indians of northern California spun tales of the giant *Loo-Poo-oi'-yes* ("Old Man of Rock"), who inhabited the neighborhood of present-day Chowchilla, and the *Ka'-Lum-me* ("rock giant") of Putah Creek (in Yolo and Solano Counties). Both had stony skin, with normal flesh beneath, and dwelled in caves.[1]

Preposterous? Perhaps—but what, then, shall we make of the 12-foot-tall skeleton excavated by soldiers digging a powder magazine near Lompoc, in Santa Barbara County, during 1833? Aside from its surprising height, the skeleton possessed a double row of teeth and lay surrounded by artifacts including stone axes, carved seashells, and blocks of porphyry etched with incomprehensible symbols. Local tribesmen gathered to view the skeleton with awe, whereupon it was reburied and subsequently "lost."[2]

A half-century later, in 1885, a party of prospectors explored the landscape around Bridalveil Fall, in Mariposa County's Yosemite Valley. At one stop, group leader G.F. Martindale noticed a heap of stones at the base of a cliff and ordered his men to dismantle it. Behind the rock pile they found a manmade wall of stones, meticulously carved so that none varied more than one-eighth of an inch in size from its neighbors. Propelled by curiosity, the miners hammered through that wall and found a tomb of sorts, carved into the mountainside. The vault measured 9 feet 3 inches tall, 8 feet 4 inches wide, and 18 feet 6 inches deep. Within lay the "fossil bones of a giant mummy," wrapped in animal skins and dusted with an unidentified gray powder. Upon unwrapping their prize, the miners found that the crude shroud actually contained *two* corpses—a female 6 feet 8 inches tall, clutching an infant to her withered breast.[3]

The mummies were allegedly transported to Los Angeles, where unnamed "men, considered to be of great science in those days... agreed that is was a 'relic' from a race that must have inhabited this country long before the American Indian." The rest, regrettably, is silence. No trace of the mummies now remains.[4]

The Ojai Vampire

This rumored fiend belongs more properly to study of the paranormal than cryptozoology, but its legend clearly qualifies as monstrous. According to that tale—or tales—a European vampire came from Italy or Spain in 1890, to reside at Ojai, in Ventura County. Initially, it preyed on livestock, but the vampire's bodyguard—a huge black dog, on par with Britain's phantom canids dating from Medieval times—was less discreet, sometimes attacking local human residents. The outraged populace eventually tracked the hell-hound to its master's grave, routed the dog with holy water, and hammered a stake through the vampire's heart in true Hollywood style. It is impossible to date the Ojai legend, but Bram Stoker's *Dracula* was published three years prior to the vampire's alleged arrival in California. Modern rumors claim that the night-prowler's stone sarcophagus, complete with grinning skull inside, may still be found somewhere in Camp Comfort Park, off Creek Road, but no evidence supports the claim.[5]

Lizard People

Did lizard men dig vast tunnels under Los Angeles? *Courtesy of William Rebsamen*

Reptiles of humanoid appearance have featured in horror films since 1954, when *The Creature from the Black Lagoon* first surfaced on a Hollywood backlot tricked out to resemble the Amazon jungle. Two decades before that screen premier, however, California residents already were familiar with reports of lizard men at large.

The tale begins in Los Angeles, during summer 1932, when mining engineer G. Warren Shufelt began prospecting for oil, gold, and other subterranean treasures. According to the legend, he employed "a radio-directed apparatus" of his own invention, sensitive to precious minerals. Instead of striking paydirt, though, Shufelt allegedly discovered a network of tunnels beneath the city, spreading outward from the site of L.A.'s Central Library on Fifth Street, winding off in various directions toward Mount Washington (northeast of downtown), to suburban Pasadena's Southwest Museum, and to a point 20 miles offshore in Santa Monica Bay.[6]

Shufelt drew a map of the tunnel complex, based on his surface readings, and proclaimed discovery of gold deposits in some of the underground chambers. Other tunnels, he surmised, held personal belongings of a vanished race, along with stockpiles of "imperishable herbs" used as food. During the mapping process, Shufelt met a Hopi Indian, Chief Little Green Leaf, who spun a tale of prehistoric meteor showers that brought "lizard people" to Earth. According to the chief, those stranded visitors built vast cities beneath the Pacific Ocean, for which Shufelt's tunnels served as emergency retreats during times of hardship. Shufelt swallowed it whole and lobbied for funding to excavate the underground "city."[7]

On February 21, 1933, L.A. County's Board of Supervisors granted Shufelt and two partners—Ray Martin and Rex McCreary—a permit to dig for buried treasure. It was a no-risk deal for local politicians, since the seekers bore all costs and promised half of any loot recovered to the government. The first agreement allowed excavation of a 50-foot shaft, but a new deal, granted on March 27, extended the dig based on Shufelt's estimate that the still-undiscovered labyrinth was 1,900 feet long, with rooms spanning some 9,000 square feet. By late November 1933, the diggers had reached 200 feet and found nothing. Still, Shufelt vowed to press on, drilling to a depth of 1,000 feet if need be.[8]

On January 29, 1934, as one shaft reached 250 feet, the *Los Angeles Times* broke the story of Shufelt's "Lost Land of the Lizard People." Not only were the late inhabitants reptilian, Shufelt proclaimed, but their city was laid out in the *shape* of a lizard, with its "key room" buried deep beneath the intersection of Second Street and South Broadway. When that chamber was breached, he declared, it would reveal "historical gold record tablets" four feet long and 14 inches wide, explaining mankind's origins and solving other mysteries, including the disappearance of the Mayan race in the ninth century. Shufelt suspected the tunnels were flooded, but promised that divers would plumb the icy depths in search of treasure.[9]

Publicity did Shufelt's cause no good. After exposure in the *Times,* his dig was soon abandoned, and the shafts were filled in by March 5, 1934. In December 1947, one Arche Dunning, speaking for the L.A. Chamber of Commerce, told reporters, "It is quite possible, of course, that the supposed labyrinth really exists. But in view of the fact that the overlaying area is the immediate Civic Center area where an important building program is to be carried out, including federal, state, county and city building, there is little probability of any further excavations." Debate persists, surrounding the elusive tunnels and a supposed "reptilian relic"—said to be a silver medallion "depicting a full-bodied dragon"—found somewhere in Los Angeles by an unidentified "Mr. G.," sometime in 1954.[10]

From Los Angeles, the reptoid legend made a leap to Mount Shasta, 800 miles to the north. Author Stanford Cleland forged the link in July 1947, when he summarized Shufelt's adventure for *Amazing Stories* magazine, adding a claim that lizard people had been sighted twice around Mount Shasta, in Siskiyou County. On balance, it appears that the supposed Shasta sightings may have been confused with reports of cave-dwelling "Lemurians"—survivors of an alleged island civilization in the Indian Ocean that sank, a lá Atlantis, during prehistoric times. Lemurians were also popular with readers of *Amazing Stories,* but the Shasta link appears to have its roots in a book titled *A Dweller on Two Planets,* published by Frederic Oliver in 1894. Science-fiction author Robert Heinlein revamped the myth in his 1941 short story "Lost Legacy."[11]

Mysterious Mount Shasta. *Courtesy of US Geological Survey*

The Beast of Billiwhack

Various states—including Maryland, Kentucky, and Texas—logged sightings of horned, cloven-hoofed humanoids in the twentieth century. Generically labeled "goatmen," these creatures resemble the satyrs of classical mythology, and are sometimes lumped with Bigfoot in cryptozoological literature, on the theory that witnesses may have seen an unknown primate and mistaken it for something even more bizarre.

Tales of California's goatman surfaced during World War II, when Swiss immigrant and Harvard graduate August Rübel allegedly undertook bizarre experiments for the Office of Strategic Services (forerunner of the Central Intelligence Agency) at his now-defunct Billiwhack Dairy near Santa Paula, in Ventura County. Legend casts Rübel as a kind of patriotic Dr. Frankenstein, toiling in his dairy's basement—or, perhaps, in one of his nearby gold mines—to create half-human "super soldiers" for America's war effort. In truth, Rübel joined the American Field Service—a civilian medical unit—when the U.S. entered combat with the Axis Powers, and he died in Tunisia, in 1943, when his ambulance struck a landmine. Reality, however, has little influence on legend.[12]

Although supposedly created in the 1940s, the Beast of Billiwhack waited a decade to choose its first victim, a nine-year-old boy who claimed that a white-haired monster, half man and half goat, had mauled him near Rübel's dairy, leaving scratches on his arms and back. Sightings continued thereafter, generally reported by children or teenagers like the one whom sheriff's deputies caught in 1964, prowling the Rübel property with sword in hand, hoping to slay the beast. The last known sighting was recorded in 1992.[13]

One possible solution for the mystery lies in the 1939 sightings of "a strange half monkey, half man" around Ojai, some 15 miles from the Billiwhack Dairy. One witness, Catherine Loughboro, told police that the beast stole two of her chickens. Another, Mrs. Tom Richards, claimed that she saw it eat corn in her field. No mention was made at the time of horns, claws, or albino fur. The Ojai sightings properly belong to California Bigfoot lore, and likely paved the way for what followed.[14]

Char Man

Ghosts have no place in cryptozoology, but stories of Ventura County's malevolent "Char Man" suggest that he—or it—may be a scarred and deranged survivor of a brush fire that ravaged Ojai Valley in 1948. Since then, local residents claim, the blackened relic of humanity has frightened motorists and hikers along Creek Road. Ojai police suggest an alternate solution, referring to a reclusive and unidentified skin-cancer victim who treasured his privacy, passing his final years as a hermit, glimpsed on occasion while walking his dog along rural highways.[15]

Char Man's legend has a cinematic counterpart in *The Prey* (1984), a horror film depicting campers in the Colorado Rockies stalked by a hideous killer. The "monster," portrayed by seven-foot-tall Dutch actor Carel Struycken, turns out to be a scarred forest-fire survivor who craves female companionship at any cost.[16]

El Chupacabra

The chupacabra ("goat sucker," in Spanish) is a mysterious blood-drinking predator first reported from Puerto Rico, where it was dubbed the "Moca Vampire" in 1975, then christened with its current name when attacks resumed in 1991. Despite its label, the creature's prey has never been restricted to goats. It also snacks on horses, sheep, dogs, rabbits, poultry—and, if we accept the stories of alleged chupacabra survivors, on the occasional human.[17]

After terrorizing Puerto Rico for six years, the chupacabra or something like it surfaced in Latin America, raiding farmyards in Guatemala, Mexico, Costa Rica, Brazil, Argentina, Chile, and Nicaragua through the latter 1990s and into the twenty-first century. The first alleged attacks on U.S. soil were reported from Miami in March 1996, followed closely by incidents in Arizona, Texas, and California. At the same time, claims emerged of chupacabras killing sheep in Spain and Portugal.[18]

While many witnesses claim chupacabra sightings, no consistent description of the creature(s) exists. Some observers say that it vaguely resembles a dog, thus indirectly supporting official claims that most "chupa" raids are the work of wild or domestic canids. Other witnesses describe winged beasts or waddling apelike figures. The "classic" description refers to a bipedal creature of somewhat reptilian appearance, with clawed "hands" on its forelegs, long fangs, and a row of sharp spines running down its back. In Nicaragua, where hunters supposedly killed a chupacabra in 2000, official reports described it as "a common dog." Another was shot in Chile, that same year, but the necropsy report was allegedly suppressed by "unidentified agencies."[19]

Many witnesses claim sightings of the predatory chupacabra. *Courtesy of William Rebsamen*

California recorded its first chupacabra sightings in May 1996. Witness Roberto Garcia was dozing in his Orange County home, beside an open window, when he woke to the pain of fangs piercing his hand. Bolting upright, he glimpsed "a sizable, shadowy figure" retreating into darkness. Around the same time, and 240 miles to the north in Fresno County, some unseen prowler killed a rooster and drained its blood.[20]

A report widely posted on the Internet claims that the chupacabra also struck in Poway, a suburb of San Diego, during June 1996. According to a June 30 story from the *Advocate Herald,* "Recent sightings and a reported attack have put the entire community on alert. City officials, however, claim to know nothing about the events that have the local residents locking their doors and closing their windows at night." Strangely, despite multiple online citations, exhaustive searches reveal no *Advocate Herald* published in California, either currently or in the past. Poway's local newspaper is the *Poway News Chieftan*.[21]

In 1997, Texas resident Joyce Murphy ran an article on the chupacabra in her *Beyond Boundaries* newsletter, which elicited a letter from an unidentified resident of Hesperia, in California's San Bernardino County. After discussing UFO sightings at nearby Phelan, the letter reported decimation of the local coyote population by some unknown predator, then proceeded to describe a December 6 attack on the correspondent's property. It read:

> Last month, my pig was going nuts outside. I looked out and didn't see anything but she was going crazy squealing. As a reenactment educator I am handy with a sword and so I went outside with it. I encountered something trying to get to my pig that was unbelievable. When I came around the corner it stopped and looked up at me. My dogs were barking under my house and when they realized I was out there they came out and moved toward this thing. They seemed to be afraid of it until I was there to back them up. The thing looked at them and then at me and seemed to be afraid of the sword that I was carrying. I had the sword in a striking position, the dogs charged the creature, and it took off behind the house jumping our three foot fence that sags in the middle. It then disappeared into the bushes. The dogs chased it to the fence, stopped, and came back. I think they were too afraid to go after it.[22]

Murphy wrote back, requesting further details and a full description of the predator. While fearing dismissal as "a nut," the Hesperian acknowledged further sightings and supplied the following details:

> As to what we have seen, it usually appears after dark, and recently not as often. This creature stands on two legs and is a dark smokey grey [*sic*]. It seems to be covered by a sort of peach type fuzz in the same grey color. The eyes are enormous almond shaped. My husband saw this thing first and in the dark the eyes appeared to be black. A few days ago I had an amazing encounter with one and the eyes appeared much lighter, almost fasceted [*sic*] to me. They were light as well as reflecting the nearby lights in their depths. The head is an oval shape that is much wider on the top. The arms have three digets [*sic*] that have very long claws on the ends they connect at the shoulders. The arms themselves

are very thin and give the appearance of limited power, and yet we watched in fascination as it tore open the chainlink of the pigpen almost effortlessly. From some angles it resembled a mini person about three to four feet tall approximately 75 to 80 pounds. When it walks it has a slumped over gait. The one time my husband went after it at the pigpen he noticed these spikey things on its back like porcupine quills that seemed to move independently. When he got close they began to twitch and he was thoroughly convinced that this thing could launch them if he chose to.[23]

Internet reporter Sam Zaydel published an article in June 1997, referring to multiple sightings from an unnamed "small town near San Diego." While directly quoting one line from the supposed *Advocate Herald* article of June 1996, he went on to write:

People also said that the creature is able to fly, more like to hop pretty far, about 25 feet, and more, and it seems like the creature could change its color at night, it changes to really dark, grey perhaps, at daytime a sunlight color is used. It has been reported to have attacked both humans and livestock. This is something new, and it alerts everybody, because this is the first time it attacked a large mammal, that is human [*sic*]. People are in panic, closing their doors, and windows at night. Do scientists have an answer to the question what is this small violent thing[?] Some scientists believe that this small carnivorous thing is another experiment, just like that with killer bees....I think that scientists try to cover something up. Why? Because if you examine the bites the creatures make, you will find that the creature is intelligent. The sharp teeth of the creature cut through the neck right into the brain and relieve the victim from any kind of pain. This kind of bite also eliminates the amount of blood loss. Which means that the creature knows what it is doing, and how, it also makes the creature more dangerous.[24]

On balance, Zaydel's sensational report appears to be an elaboration of the untraceable *Advocate Herald* piece, moved forward in time and devoid of supporting documentation.

If California's chupacabra is seldom seen in the flesh, it can be found more easily on liquor store shelves. In 2006, the L.A.-based Merkin Vineyards and its associated Caduceus Cellars winery introduced a red wine labeled Chupacabra, selling for $27.99 per bottle. As advertised, it represents: "The Trickster. The Shape Shifter. The ever elusive shadow who mutates with the Sun and Moon. One year a Dragon, another a Snake. This is our Mystery blend. Think forest, not trees. Think weather, not rain. Stare and the CHUPACABRA, who dwells in your heart and not in your head, will vanish. Only a True Alchemist can draw holy blood from a stone, and the CHUPACABRA is his opus, his phoenix, his cherub, his child."[25]

Two years later, in summer 2008, a chupacabra "flap" engulfed Yucca Valley, in San Bernardino County. Various locals reported sightings of "a spotted, short-haired dog-like creature" in the neighborhood, and while it evaded pursuers, officials had a ready explanation. Melanie Crider, manager of the town's animal control department, told the *Hi-Desert Star,* "We have seen, over the years, coyotes with mange so bad that it looks like leprosy. It's a sad part of nature, but these diseased animals can survive a long time in this condition."[26]

While true believers reject such mundane diagnoses, medical tests performed on three alleged chupacabras killed in Texas between 2004 and 2007 revealed that all were malnourished coyotes disfigured by sarcoptic mange, a highly contagious infestation of burrowing mites that produces extensive hair loss, accompanied by skin damage from incessant biting and scratching.[27]

The *good* news, for those who believe, is that classic chupacabras bear no resemblance to dogs, bald or otherwise. Like the strange beast reported from Hesperia in 1996, they belong in a class all their own.

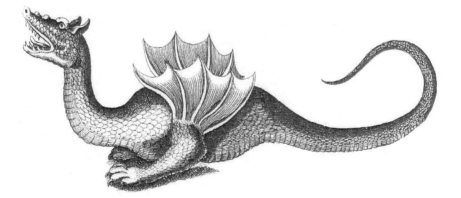

Conclusion

Most books collecting tales of unknown creatures are outdated before they reach print. New sightings emerge weekly—or daily, in some areas—while ongoing archival research uncovers more historical reports each year. In California, where unusual events and monstrous encounters are almost routine, the book is never closed on mysterious phenomenon. No author has the last word.

Sadly, no central clearinghouse exists for California "monsters." Ray Crowe's International Bigfoot Society filled that gap for many years, at least where Sasquatch sightings were concerned, but age and failing health have written finis to a lifetime of energetic field research. Ray's long-running Track Record newsletter ceased publication in 2007, and May 2008 brought news that an organization calling itself the North America Bigfoot Search (NABS) had purchased his archives. Ray's invaluable website, detailing hundreds of Bigfoot sightings nationwide, remained online until spring 2009, when it vanished literally overnight in circumstances that remain obscure. Web browsers, for now, are connecting searchers to a Seattle-based group, the Sasquatch Information Society, but unfortunately Crowe's files and library seem to have vanished—at least for the present and little information about sightings is available.

In the absence of a reliable and/or responsive archive, readers of Strange California Monsters are invited to report their sightings of Bigfoot—or any other cryptid—directly to this author, either via Schiffer Books or preferably at the website, www.michaelnewton.homestead.com. All information is welcome. Enquiries shall be answered as time and this thing called Life permit.

The search continues.

Endnotes

Introduction

1. Peter Costello, *The Magic Zoo.* London: Sphere, 1979.
2. Newton, *Encyclopedia of Cryptozoology,* p. 3.
3. BCSCC, http://www.bcscc.ca; CFZ, http://www.cfz.org.uk.
4. Newton, p. 3.
5. Chad Arment, *Cryptozoology: Science & Speculation* (Landisville, PA: Coachwhip, 2004), p. 16.

Chapter 1

1. Counting California, http://countingcalifornia.cdlib.org.
2. Ibid.
3. Geography of California, Wikipedia, http://en.wikipedia.org/wiki/Geography_of_ California.
4. Ibid.
5. List of U.S. Wilderness Areas, Wikipedia, http://en.wikipedia.org/wiki/List_of_U.S._ Wilderness_Areas.
6. Sanderson, *Abominable Snowmen,* pp. 100-102.
7. Ibid.
8. "Giant waterfall discovered in California."
9. California Department of Fish and Game (hereafter CDFG), http://www.dfg. ca.gov.
10. Santschi, "Wild parrots ruffle feathers in Redlands."
11. Krieger and Goldston, "Mystery bird."
12. U.S. Geological Survey, http://nas.er.usgs.gov/queries/FactSheet. asp?speciesID=419; "Relative of piranha found in California lake."
13. Channidae, Wikipedia, http://en.wikipedia.org/ wiki/Channidae; Internet Movie Data Base.
14. Channidae, Wikipedia; Snakehead Stories, U.S. Fish & Wildlife Service, http:// www.fws.gov/snakehead3.htm.
15. California condor, Wikipedia, http://en.wikipedia.org/wiki/California_Condor; Endangered Species in California, http://www.endangeredspecie.com/states/ ca.htm.
16. Brown Bear, Wikipedia, http://en.wikipedia.org/wiki/Brown_bear; Stienstra, "Sighting suggests bears are present."
17. Orin Starn, *Ishi's Brain.* New York: W.W. Norton, 2004.
18. Ibid.
19. "Bizarre new jellyfish discovered." *New Scientist,* May 7, 2003.
20. "New species of underwater bone-eating worm found." ABC News, July 30, 2004.
21. "California: Scientists find new species of coral." *New York Times,* Feb. 11, 2005.
22. "New species of salamander found in Siskiyou Mountains." Environmental Protection Information Center, May 16, 2005.
23. Barbassa, "Dozens of new species."

Chapter 2

1. Eberhart, p. 655.
2. Length of the U.S. Coastline by States, http:// www.teachervision.fen.com/maps/ bodies-of-water/725.html; USA Place Names, http://www.placenames.com/ us.
3. Newton, pp. 416-17.
4. Coleman and Huyghe, pp. 290-1.
5. Holder, p. 25; "Oarfish," Wikipedia, http://en.wikipedia.org/wiki/Oarfish. 30.
6. "Fishermen have battle with sea serpent." *Fort Wayne* (Ind.) *Journal Gazette,* Feb. 21, 1909.
7. LeBlond and Bousfield, p. 95.
8. Clark, p. 30.
9. *Modesto* (Calif.) *News,* May 22, 1912.
10. Coleman and Huyghe, p. 97; Garner, pp. 165-6; Heuvelmans, pp. 478-9.
11. Coleman and Huyghe, pp. 97-8; Garner, p. 166; Heuvelmans, p. 479.
12. Garner, p. 166; Heuvelmans, p. 479.
13. Garner, p. 166; Heuvelmans, p. 480.
14. Garner, pp. 166-7; Heuvelmans, p. 480.
15. Garner, p. 167; Heuvelmans, p. 480.
16. Garner, p. 167; Heuvelmans, p. 480.
17. Heuvelmans, pp. 480-1.
18. Ibid., p. 481.
19. Heuvelmans, pp. 542-3, 552-7, 581.
20. Eberhart, p. 483.
21. Heuvelmans, p. 584; Eberhart, p. 404; Old Man of Monterey Bay, Metroactive, http://www.metroactive.com/papers/cruz/09.22.99/hauntings-9938.html.
22. Eberhart, p. 404.
23. Eberhart, p. 404.
24. Fortean Bureau, http://www.forteanbureau.com/blog /archives/002017.html; Metroactive, http://www.metroactive. com/papers/cruz/09.22.99/haunt-ings-9938.html; Heuvelmans, p. 584.
25. *Lost Tapes,* Animal Planet, Dec. 19, 2008.
26. *Monterey County Herald*, www.montereyherald.com, search conducted on Dec. 21, 2008.
27. Bord and Bord, *Unexplained,* p. 359.
28. "RavenMad" on Thothweb, http://www.thothweb.com/ ftopict-1284.html (Oct. 17, 2005); Heuvelmans, p. 584.
29. Eberhart, pp. 65, 404; Heuvelmans, pp. 478, 584.
30. Eberhart, p. 65; Heuvelmans, p. 478.
31. Bord and Bord, *Unexplained,* p. 358.
32. Keel, pp. 292-3.
33. Ibid., p. 293.
34. Heuvelmans, p. 588.
35. Garner, p. 163; KGO-TV Channel 7, San Francisco, Sept. 7, 2006.
36. KGO-TV Channel 7, San Francisco, Sept. 7, 2006.
37. Garner, p. 164.
38. Garner, pp. 164-5; LeBlond and Bousfield, p. 115.
39. Ellis, p. 29.

40. "'Sea serpents' seen off California coast." *International Society of Cryptozoology Newsletter*, 2 (Winter 1983): 9; Bord and Bord, p. 359; Ellis, p. 29.

41. SF Sea Serpent, http://home.access4less.net/~sfseaserpent/index.html.

42. Ibid.

43. Ibid.

44. Ibid.

45. Ibid.

46. Ibid.

47. Ibid.; BSM Associates, http://smtp.antelecom.net/blogs/BSMA/item_71.htm; Out of Place Artifacts, http:// www.s8int.com/noahsark9.html; The TalkOrigins Archive, http://www.talkorigins.org/faqs/credentials.html.

48. Champagne, pp. 1, 11.

49. Charles Skinner, *American Myths and Legends* (Philadelphia: Lippincott, 1903), pp. 275-6.

50. Roland Dixon, "Water monsters in northern California." *Journal of American Folklore* 19 (1906): 323.

51. "Lake Elizabeth," Wikipedia, http://en.wikipedia. org/wiki/Elizabeth_Lake_(California).

52. Lake Elizabeth Monster, http://www.globide.com/ forum/index. php?showtopic=675; WrightwoodCalif.com, http://www.wrightwoodcalif. com/forum/index.php?topic=10310.0;prev_next=next.

53. Lake Elizabeth Monster; WrightwoodCalif.com; Eberhart, p. 680.

54. Lake Elizabeth Monster; WrightwoodCalif.com; Horace Bell, *On the Old West Coast* (New York: William Morrow, 1930), pp. 198-206.

55. Jason Song, "At a remote forest lake, a monstrous legend spawns." *Los Angeles Times,* Jan. 6, 2001.

56. Hector Lee, *Heroes, Villains and Ghosts: Folklore of Old California* (Santa Barbara: Capra Press, 1984), pp. 151-5.

57. Clark, pp. 21-2; USA Place Names.

58. Clark, p. 21.

59. Clark, p. 22; USA Place Names.

60. "Lake Elsinore," Wikipedia, http://en.wikipedia.org/wiki/Lake_Elsinore,_California.

61. Eberhart, p. 229; "Times past," *Los Angeles Times,* Sept. 13, 2006.

62. "Lake Elsinore," Wikipedia.

63. Kirk, pp. 171-2.

64. Kirk, p. 172; Loren Coleman, "Lake Elsinore monster bobs up again," Cryptomundo, http://www.cryptomundo.com/cryptozoo-news/elsie/ (Aug. 15, 2006).

65. "Lake Tahoe," Wikipedia, http://en.wikipedia.org/wiki/Lake_Tahoe.

66. Skinner, *American Myths and Legends,* pp. 283-4; Rocha.

67. Rocha.

68. Eberhart, p. 533.

69. Kirk, pp. 155-6.

70. Sheffield; Stienstra.

71. Yahoo! Travel, http://travel.yahoo.com/p-travelguide-2837363-tahoe_tessie_s_lake_tahoe_monster_museum_south_lake_tahoe-i.

72. The Lake Hodges Monster.

73. Krier; The Lake Hodges Monster; Tapia.

74. The Lake Hodges Monster; Tapia.

75. The Lake Hodges Monster.

76. Ibid.
77. The Lake Hodges Monster; Tapia.
78. Krier; The Lake Hodges Monster; Tapia.
79. Ibid.
80. Ibid.
81. The Lake Hodges Monster.
82. Coleman, *Mysterious America,* pp. 93-4; USA Place Names; "Lost River," Wiki-pedia, http://en.wikipedia.org/wiki/Lost_River_(California).
83. Coleman, *Mysterious America,* pp. 93-4.
84. "Mekong giant catfish," Wikipedia, http://en. wikipedia.org/wiki/Pangasius_gigas#Size; "Wels catfish," Wikipedia, http://en.wikipedia.org/wiki/Wels_catfish; Gordon McHenry, "Giant catfish setting records," http://www.katmasters.com/news/a23.html.
85. FindLakes, http://findlakes.com/stafford_lake_ california~ca00321.htm; "'Sea monster' captured," *New York Times,* Aug. 25, 1984.
86. Eberhart, p. 110.
87. Eberhart, p. 110; USA Place Names.

Chapter 3

1. "Amphibian," Wikipedia, http://en.wikipedia.org/wiki/Amphibian.
2. "Reptile," Wikipedia, http://en.wikipedia.org/wiki/Reptile.
3. "Cold-blooded," Wikipedia, http://en.wikipedia.org/wiki/Cold-blooded.
4. California Dept. of Fish and Game (hereafter CDFG), http://www.dfg.ca.gov/bio-geodata/cwhr/pdfs/species_ list.pdf.
5. "Salamander," Wikipedia, http://en.wikipedia.org/wiki/Salamander; CDFG; Steb-bins, p. 38.
6. Coleman, *Tom Slick,* p. 120; Coleman and Huyghe, p. 232; USA Place Names.
7. Coleman, *Tom Slick,* p. 120; Coleman and Huyghe, pp. 232-3.
8. Myers.
9, Ibid.
10. Coleman, *Tom Slick,* p. 123; Coleman and Huyghe, pp. 233-4.
11. Coleman, *Tom Slick,* pp. 124-5; Coleman and Huyghe, p. 234.
12. Coleman, *Tom Slick,* p. 124; Coleman and Huyghe, p. 234; Rogers.
13. Coleman and Huyghe, pp. 234-5, 312; USA Place Names.
14. "Crocodilia," Wikipedia, http://en.wikipedia.org/wiki/Crocodilia; CDFG.
15. Coleman, *Mysterious America,* p. 300; Bord and Bord, *Unexplained,* p. 360.
16. Coleman, *Mysterious America,* p. 302; Bord and Bord, *Unexplained,* p. 360.
17. Bord and Bord, *Unexplained,* p. 220.
18. Coleman, *Mysterious America,* pp. 276, 304; USA Place Names.
19. Coleman, *Mysterious America,* p. 304.
20. Littlejohn, "It's gator vu."
21. "The 'monster' of Loch Chabot"; Phillips.
22. "Gator captured."
23. Littlejohn, "Machado Lake closes"; Littlejohn, "Gator watch"; Gresko; Powers, "Hunting the Monster."
24. Littlejohn, "City and wranglers"; Littlejohn, "Is there room"; Littlejohn, "Officials say"; Malcolm; "'Stressed' gator"; "Police arrest two"; Thermos; "Firefighters capture alligator"; Gregor.

25. Martinez; "Gator surfaces"; Pool; "L.A.'s Reggie."
26. CDFG; Stebbins, p. 97.
27. "News from around Southern California," *San Jose Mercury News*, Sept. 10, 2004.
28. "News from around Southern California"; "Alligator snapping turtle," Wikipedia, http://en.wikipedia.org/wiki/Alligator_snapping_turtle.
29. "News from around Southern California"; "Alligator snapping turtle."
30. CDFG; Stebbins, pp. 169-70; "Monitor lizard," Wikipedia, http://en.wikipedia.org/wiki/Monitor_lizard; Florida's Exotic Wildlife, http://myfwc.com/nonnatives/exotics/SpeciesNumberResults.asp?SPPNO=291.
31. "A gigantic lizard." *Woodland Daily Democrat,* Aug. 8, 1891.
32. Hunter; Zieralski.
33. CDFG; Stebbins, p. 189.
34. Arment, *Boss Snakes,* pp. 88-92.
35. Ibid., p. 91.
36. Ibid., p. 92.
37. Ibid., pp. 87-8.
38. Ibid., p. 88; Stebbins, pp. 173-4.
39. Arment, *Boss Snakes,* p. 88.
40. Ibid., pp. 92-3.
41. Ibid., p. 92.
42. Ibid., pp. 93-5.
43. "Big Serpent Seen Again."
44. Arment, *Boss Snakes*, pp. 95-6.
45. Ibid., pp. 96-7.
46. Ibid., pp. 97-8.
47. Ibid., pp. 98-9.
48. Paul Roberts, "River serpent," *Fortean Times* no. 128 (November 1999): 52; "The 'monster' of Loch Chabot."
49. "Florida's python problem," ABC News, June 14, 2006; Jörg Blech, "Burmese pythons invade Florida," *Spiegel,* Dec. 22, 2006, at http://www.spiegel.de/international/spiegel/0,1518,456018,00.html.

Chapter 4

1. California Bird List of the Western Field Ornithologists' California Bird Records Committee, Jan. 27, 2008, http://www.wfo-cbrc.org/cbrc/ca_list.html.
2. "California condor," Wikipedia, http://en.wikipedia.org/wiki/California_Condor.
3. "Golden eagle," Wikipedia, http://en.wikipedia.org/wiki/Golden_Eagle.
4. "Bald eagle," Wikipedia, http://en.wikipedia.org/wiki/Bald_Eagle.
5. "Turkey vulture," Wikipedia, http://en.wikipedia.org/wiki/Turkey_Vulture.
6. Hall, *Thunderbirds,* pp. 66-7; Clinton Hart Merriam, Wikipedia, http://en.wikipedia.org/wiki/Clinton_Hart_Merriam.
7. C. Hart Merriam, *The Dawn of the World* (Cleveland: Arthur Clark, 1910), p. 163.
8. Riley Woodford, "Eagle flight and other myths," Alaska Dept. of Fish & Game, http://www.wildlifenews. alaska.gov/index.cfm?adfg=wildlife_news.view_article&issue_id=58&articles_id=343.
9. Hall, *Thunderbirds,* p. 72.

10. Hall, *Thunderbirds,* p. 36-7; Ivanpah, http://www. ghosttowns.com/states/ca/ivanpah.html.
11. Hall, *Thunderbirds,* pp. 37-8.
12. Ibid., pp. 38-9.
13. Hall, *Thunderbirds,* pp. 39-40; "Teratornithidae," Wikipedia, http://en.wikipedia. org/wiki/Teratornithidae.
14. "Teratornithidae," Wikipedia.
15. Clark, pp. 16-17.
16. Ibid.
17. "Weird, weird rain," About.com, http://paranormal .about.com/library/weekly/aa082602a.htm; Bobette Bryan, "Strange rain," http://www.underworldtales.com/strange.htm.
18. Quoted in Clark, pp. 17-18.
19. Coghlan, *Dictionary of Cryptozoology,* p. 83.
20. Quoted in Arment, "Pterodactyls of Fresno County."
21. Ibid.
22. Ibid.
23. "Chrysopelea," Wikipedia, http://en.wikipedia. org/wiki/Chrysopelea; "Draco (genus)," Wikipedia, http:// en.wikipedia.org/wiki/Draco_lizard.
24. Keel, pp. 243-4.
25. Ibid.
26. Ibid.
27. Ibid.
28. Ibid.
29. IBS #159, 2262.
30. Ibid.

Chapter 5

1. "Big cat," Wikipedia, http://en.wikipedia.org/wiki/Big_cat.
2. "Jaguar," Wikipedia, http://en.wikipedia.org/wiki/Jaguar.
3. Newton, pp. 16-17.
4. "Cougar," Wikipedia, http://en.wikipedia.org/ wiki/Cougar.
5. Quoted in Coleman, *Mysterious America,* p. 137.
6. Ibid.
7. Ibid., p. 138.
8. "Mr. Ashworth killes large California lion," *Union Democrat* (Sonora, CA), November 18, 1854; "Another story about that extraordinary California hunter," *New York Times,* March 1, 1873.
9. Covarrubias; Griggs; Mackey; Pringle.
10. Griggs; Hernandez; Mackey; Pringle; "Suspected lion."
11. Griggs; Hernandez; Mackey.
12. "'Animal' seen not lion"; Griggs.
13. Covarrubias; Wides.
14. Covarrubias; Wides.
15. Covarrubias.
16. "Valley Center, California," Wikipedia, http://en. wikipedia.org/wiki/Valley_Center,_California.
17. "Reports of tiger sighting leads to fruitless search."

18. Ibid.
19. "Fremont, California," Wikipedia, http://en.wikipedia.org/wiki/Fremont,_California.
20. Coleman, *Mysterious America,* p. 127; Shuker, *Mystery Cats of the World,* p. 168.
21. Coleman, *Mysterious America,* pp. 127-8.
22. Ibid.
23. Ibid., p. 296.
24. "Black panther," Wikipedia, http://en.wikipedia.org/wiki/Black_panther.
25. Coleman, *Mysterious America,* pp. 118, 296.
26. Ibid., pp. 118-19, 296.
27. Ibid., pp. 120-1.
28. Ibid., p. 121.
29. Ibid.
30. Ibid., pp. 120-1.
31. Ibid., p. 196.
32. Stienstra, "Hills are alive."
33. Stienstra, "Mysterious black panther."
34. Ibid.
35. Kovner.
36. Stienstra, "'Black panther sightings.'"
37. "Black panther," Wikipedia; Coleman, *More Strange Highways,* pp. 43-8; Stienstra, "'Black panther sightings'"; Stienstra, "Hills are alive."
38. "Black panther," Wikipedia.
39. Eastern Puma Research Network; "Alabama panther or just a black cougar?" Cryptozoology.com, http://www. cryptozoology.com/forum/topic_view_thread. php?tid=3&pid=521117.
40. Stienstra, "'Black panther sightings.'"
41. Coleman, *Mysterious America,* pp. 150-4; "American lion," Wikipedia, http://en.wikipedia.org/wiki/American_ Lion.

Chapter 6

1. Green, p. 6; Murphy, pp. 8, 25-8; Bord and Bord, *Bigfoot,* pp. 171-310; Bord and Bord, *Unexplained,* pp. 357-60; BFRO website; GCBRO website; IBS website.
2. Newton, *Encyclopedia,* p. 412; Eberhart, pp. 101, 300, 306, 336, 403-4, 534, 552, 560; IBS #4154.
3. "California," Wikipedia; IBS #4154.
4. "California," Wikipedia; Arment, *Historical Bigfoot,* p. 93.
5. USA Place Names; Bigfoot Encounters.
6. Bord and Bord, *Bigfoot,* p. 12; Green, p. 42.
7. Bord and Bord, *Bigfoot,* pp. 12-13; Green, pp. 42-3.
8. Arment, *Historical,* pp. 93-4; Bord and Bord, *Bigfoot,* p. 220.
9. Arment, *Historical,* pp. 97-8; Green, pp. 43-4.
10. Bord and Bord, *Bigfoot,* p. 220.
11. Arment, *Historical,* p. 98; IBS #327, 373, 395.
12. Arment, *Historical,* pp. 99-101; IBS #1115 and 3896.
13. Arment, *Historical,* p. 104; Bigfoot Encounters; Bord and Bord, *Bigfoot,* pp. 23-4, 222.

14. Bord and Bord, *Bigfoot,* p. 28; Arment, *Historical,* pp. 105-6.

15. IBS #2060; USA Place Names; BFRO #8059.

16. Arment, *Historical,* pp. 106-7; IBS #669 and 330.

17. Bord and Bord, *Bigfoot,* p. 49; Green, p. 306.

18. IBS #713, 3132 and 3892; BFRO #2896 and 8059; Bord and Bord, *Bigfoot,* pp. 54, 230.

19. IBS #1167, 1620, 1694, and 3940.

20. BFRO #2428 and 3684; IBS #4140; Clark and Coleman, p. 89.

21. BFRO #1301; Bigfoot Encounters; Bord and Bord, *Bigfoot,* pp. 59-61, 231; Green, pp. 344-6.

22. IBS #967, 2917, 2919 and 3432.

23. BFRO #528, 1229 and 4946.

24. Green, pp. 65-7.

25. Green, pp. 67-9; IBS #326, 328, 329, 330, 333, 1140, 1761, 1988, 1989 and 2920.

26. Newton, p. 481.

27. Ibid., pp. 481-2; Coleman, *Bigfoot!,* pp. 71-80.

28. Bord and Bord, *Bigfoot,* pp. 235-57; BFRO; GCBRO; IBS.

29. Bord and Bord, *Bigfoot,* pp. 235-57; BFRO; GCBRO; IBS.

30. IBS #2634; GCBRO.

31. IBS #1795.

32. Bord and Bord, *Bigfoot,* p. 238.

33. Bord and Bord, *Bigfoot,* pp. 239-40; IBS #1611, 1684; BFRO #1953, 7759.

34. Clark and Coleman, p. 112; IBS #751, 2500, 3182; Bord and Bord, *Bigfoot,* pp. 241, 243.

35. Green, p. 307.

36. Bord and Bord, *Bigfoot,* pp. 87-8, 244-5; BFRO #8059.

37. Bord and Bord, *Bigfoot,* pp. 103-4, 248-9; BFRO #2876, 2907.

38. Bord and Bord, *Bigfoot,* pp. 107-8, 253, 255-6.

39. Bigfoot Encounters; IBS #2556.

40. Bord and Bord, *Bigfoot,* pp. 257-307; BFRO; GCBRO; IBS.

41. Bord and Bord, *Bigfoot,* pp. 257-307; BFRO; GCBRO; IBS.

42. BFRO #160, 803, 1634, 1955, 2182, 2199, 2579, 2770, 2887, 2996, 3612, 4182, 4366, 4790, 5520, 5477, 5637, 6706, 7097, 7231, 7352, 7676, 10718, 12328, 13236, 13287, 13839; GCBRO; IBS #308, 318, 364, 368, 384, 836, 914, 996, 1461, 1523, 1571, 1736, 1759, 1760, 2016, 2157, 2389, 2397, 2440, 2511, 2537, 2803, 3287, 3369, 3470.

43. BFRO #8059; Bigfoot Encounters; Bord and Bord, *Bigfoot,* pp. 117-18, 259, 285; IBS #2437.

44. IBS #1456, 1574; Bigfoot Encounters.

45. BFRO #83; IBS #1503, 2581.

46. Bigfoot Encounters; Bord and Bord, *Bigfoot,* pp. 218-310; BFRO #2708; Green, p. 315; IBS #1460.

47. BFRO #2782, 15540; Bigfoot Encounters.

48. BFRO; Bord and Bord, *Bigfoot,* pp. 171-88; GCBRO; IBS.

49. BFRO; Bord and Bord, *Bigfoot,* pp. 171-88; GCBRO; IBS.

50. BFRO #431, 816, 1058, 1548, 2142, 2150, 2228, 2333, 2888, 3424, 3605, 4445, 4886, 4929, 5104, 6521, 6971, 7336, 7773, 8184, 9426, 11407, 13613, 16550, 21684; Bigfoot Encounters; Bord and Bord, *Bigfoot,* p. 308; GCBRO; IBS #263, 562, 721, 1156, 1181, 1312, 1339, 1599, 2345, 2453, 2645, 2707, 2904, 3518, 3925.

51. BFRO #2855, 2864; IBS #723, 1217, 2553, 2615, 3147, 3997.
52. Bigfoot Encounters; GCBRO.
53. BFRO; Bigfoot Encounters; Bord and Bord, *Bigfoot,* pp. 188-98; GCBRO; IBS.
54. BFRO #97, 596, 1036, 1496, 1578, 1579, 1665, 1794, 1963, 2037, 2137, 2148, 2151, 2211, 2212, 2311, 2326, 2387, 2558, 2817, 2819, 2843, 2861, 2873, 2955, 2960, 2961, 3683, 3798, 4947, 5509, 5253, 6160, 8069, 8784, 8868, 11162, 11519, 15013; Bigfoot Encounters; GCBRO; IBS #108, 157, 158, 160, 161, 162, 163, 246, 271, 335, 492, 557, 559, 611, 631, 699, 732, 759, 788, 831, 925, 941, 1044, 1064, 1069, 1075, 1076, 1077, 1080, 1084, 1092, 1145, 1258, 1303, 1377, 2045. 2059, 2168, 2169, 2260, 2261, 2263, 2265, 2266, 2328, 2353, 2360, 2473, 2608, 2750, 2832, 2900, 2902, 3034, 3080, 3131, 3145, 3180, 3191, 3258, 3278, 3282, 3396, 3407, 3526, 3826, 3831, 3841, 3842, 3843, 3847, 3860, 4050, 4081.
55. BFRO #1579; Bigfoot Encounters; IBS #109, 112, 131, 931, 1111, 1198, 2035, 2235, 3400, 3890, 3974, 4087, 4170, 4180.
56. IBS #636, 2550, 2745, 2987, 4180.
57. BFRO #11897, 18298; Bigfoot Encounters; IBS #81, 168, 475, 1238, 2128, 2154, 2272, 2820, 3844, 4019.
58. BFRO #1557; IBS #504, 2167, 2848, 3222, 3908.
59. BFRO; Bigfoot Encounters; Bord and Bord, *Bigfoot,* pp. 199-212; GCBRO; IBS.
60. BFRO #147, 166, 369, 405, 502, 533, 802, 835, 2255, 2431, 2859, 2942, 3021, 3029, 3071, 3072, 3105, 3121, 3794, 3822, 4043, 4637, 4649, 4650, 4845, 4885, 4917, 5294, 5383, 5418, 5791, 6130, 6304, 6520, 6868, 6922, 7115, 7299, 7307, 7331, 7363, 7452, 7702, 8226, 8234, 8463, 8650, 8729, 8735, 8896, 9051, 9368, 9439, 9648, 9898, 10279, 11837, 11948, 12165, 12818, 13362, 14323, 14953, 15039, 15197, 15344, 15652, 15782, 16448, 16722, 17458, 19448, 20594, 24277; Bigfoot Encounters; GCBRO; IBS #1170, 1185, 3938, 3967, 4121, 4178, 4181.
61. BFRO #2928, 6922, 12518; Bigfoot Encounters; GCBRO; IBS #3938, 3943, 4082, 4083.
62. BFRO; Bigfoot Encounters; IBS.
63. Bigfoot Encounters; IBS #105, 197, 714, 741, 837, 1394, 1442, 1462, 1672, 1797, 1963, 2192, 2264, 2982, 3074, 3134, 3152, 3160, 3169, 3257, 3288, 3913, 4069, 4173.
64. IBS #695, 961, 965, 1078, 1191, 1285, 1744, 3074, 3845, 3968.
65. IBS #334, 632, 749, 837, 961, 1165, 1643, 1744, 1796, 2918, 2921, 2982, 3133, 3288, 3840.

Chapter 7

1. Coleman, *Bigfoot!,* pp. 81-2; Murphy and Patterson, pp. 180-1.
2. Murphy and Patterson, pp. 184-5.
3. Coleman, *Bigfoot!,* p. 82; Murphy and Patterson, pp. 184-5.
4. Murphy and Patterson, pp. 185-6.
5. Meldrum, pp. 138-43; Murphy and Patterson, pp. 186-7.
6. Murphy and Patterson, pp. 187-8.
7. Meldrum, pp. 144-5; Murphy and Patterson, pp. 188-9.
8. Murphy and Patterson, pp. 189-90.
9. Meldrum, p. 149; Murphy and Patterson, pp. 190-1.
10. Murphy and Patterson, pp. 191-2.
11. Ibid., pp. 192-3, 197.

12. Meldrum, pp. 153-4; Murphy and Patterson, p. 217.
13. Murphy and Patterson, p. 198.
14. Murphy and Patterson, p. 199.
15. Krantz, *Bigfoot Sasquatch Evidence,* pp. 116-17, 119, 304-5.
16. Murphy and Patterson, p. 201.
17. Ibid.
18. Ibid., pp. 201-2.
19. Meldrum, p. 157.
20. Ibid., pp. 157-8.
21. Murphy and Patterson, pp. 224-6.
22. Ibid., p. 221.
23. Coleman, *Bigfoot!,* p. 97.
24. Murphy and Patterson, pp. 230-1.
25. Krantz, pp. 95-6.
26. Ibid., pp. 93-120.
27. Murphy and Patterson, pp. 232-3.
28. Coleman, *Bigfoot!,* pp. 102-3; Internet Movie Database; Turner Classic Movies, http://www.tcm.com/tcmdb/ title.jsp?stid=68659&category=Overview.
29. Chorvinsky.
30. Lewis and Reid.
31. Coleman, *Bigfoot!,* p. 99.
32. Ibid., pp. 99-100.
33. Ibid., pp. 101-5.
34. Ibid., p. 105.
35. Coleman, *Bigfoot!,* pp. 105-6; Murphy and Patterson, pp. 183-264; BFRO, http://www.bfro.net/REF/hoax.asp.
36. Wasson.
37. Coleman, *Bigfoot!,* pp. 70-1; Young.
38. Long, flyleaf.
39. Ibid., pp. 10-11.
40. Greg Long address to the IBS, March 27, 2004.
41. Long, pp. 15, 29.
42. Ibid., pp. 154, 209, 443-6.
43. Ibid., pp. 344-6, 350, 355.
44. Ibid., pp. 447-53.
45. Ibid., pp. 447-53, 456-8.
46. Ibid., pp. 457-8, 460, 464.
47. Greg Long correspondence with Rich La Monica, April 4, 2004.
48. "Patterson Bigfoot film subject has been identified as human," Free Press Release (November 26, 2006), http://www.free-press-release.com/news/200611/1164583760.html; "The MK Interview on Bigfoot Live," http://txsasquatch.blogspot.com/2006/12/mk-interview-on-bigfoot-live.html.
49. Loren Coleman, "Bigfoot massacre: The theory" (May 22, 2008), http://www.cryptomundo.com/cryptozoo-news/bf-massacre.
50. Loren Coleman, "Bigfoot massacre: Naming names" (June 12, 2008), http://www.cryptomundo.com/cryptozoo-news/bluff-revisit.

Chapter 8

1. IBS #3836.
2. IBS #960, 3357.
3. Ibid.
4. Ibid.
5. Weird California, http://www.weirdca.com/location. php?location=77.
6. Stanley.
7. Ibid.
8. Ibid.
9. Ibid.
10. Ibid.
11. Walton, pp. 50-54; "Lemuria," Wikipedia, http://en.wikipedia.org/wiki/Lemuria_(continent).
12. Dager; Weird California, http://www.weirdca.com/location.php?location=76.
13. Dager; Weird California.
14. Weird California.
15. Weird California, http://www.weirdca.com/location.php?location=77.
16. "The Prey," Wikipedia, http://en.wikipedia.org/ wiki/The_Prey_(1984_film).
17. Newton, *Encyclopedia of Cryptozoology*, pp. 102-3.
18. Ibid., pp. 103-5.
19. Ibid., pp. 104-5.
20. Ibid., p. 103.
21. Chupacabras Update, http://www.io.com/~patrik/chupa3.htm; Xenophilia, http://www.xenophilia.com/zb0004b. htm; Monografie UFO, http://web.tiscali.it/lareteufo/chupa1.htm; Mondo Times, http://www.mondotimes.com/1/world/us/5/293/714.
22. Cattle Mutilations, http://www.geocities.com/Area51/Shadowlands/6583/cattle035.html.
23. Ibid.
24. Chupacabra, http://www.fortunecity.com/roswell/barker/36/main2.htm.
25. JV Wine, http://www.jvwine.com/xcart/product.php?productid=1840&cat=250&page=11.
26. Unger.
27. "Elmendorf creature wasn't part of legend," Express-News (San Antonio, TX), May 8, 2005; Jayme Blaschke, "Texas State researchers solve mystery of Cuero chupacabra," University News Service (Nov. 1, 2007), http://www.txstate.edu/news/news_releases/news_archive/2007/11/Chupacabra110107.html.

Bibliography

Abcarian, Robin. "No lie: That 'tiger' may be a liger." *Los Angeles Times,* Feb. 25, 2005.

"'Animal' seen not lion." *Monterey Herald*, Feb. 22, 2005.

Arment, Chad. *Boss Snakes.* Landisville, PA: Coachwhip Books, 2008.

—. *The Historical Bigfoot.* Landisville, PA: Coachwhip Books, 2006.

—. "The pterodactyls of Fresno County, California." *BioFortean Review* 5 (November 2006), http://www.strangeark. com/bfr/articles/pterodactyls-fresno.html.

Barbassa, Juliana. "Dozens of new species found in California national park caves." *San Jose Mercury News*, Jan. 18, 2006.

Bateman, Chris. "Archaeologist digs for proof of Sasquatch." *Union Democrat* (Sonora, CA), Jan. 26, 2007.

"Big serpent seen again." *Mendocino Democratic Daily*, Jan. 25, 1901.

Bigfoot Encounters, http://www.bigfootencounters.com/sbs/ebbetts.htm.

Bigfoot Field Researchers Organization, http://www.bfro.net.

Bord, Janet, and Colin Bord. *Alien Animals.* Harrisburg, PA: Stackpole, 1981.

—. *Bigfoot Casebook Updated.* Enumclaw, WA: Pine Winds Press, 2006.

—. *Unexplained Mysteries of the 20th Century.* Chicago: Contemporary Books, 1989.

Bringle, Paul. "Lion or tiger, not bear, oh my!" *Los Angeles Times*, Feb. 20, 2005.

Byrne, Peter. *The Search for Bigfoot.* New York: Pocket, 1976.

Cattle Mutilations, http://www.geocities.com/Area51/Shadowlands/6583/cattle035.html.

Champagne, Bruce. A Preliminary Examination of a Stabilized Video Recording of Large, Unidentified Aquatic Animals in San Francisco Bay Recorded on January 26, 2004, http://www.cryptomundo.com/wp-content/uploads/frame stabilization.pdf.

Chorvinsky, Mark. "The makeup man and the monster: John Chambers and the Patterson Bigfoot suit." *Strange Magazine* 17 (Summer 1996), http://www.strangemag.com/chambers17.html.

Chupacabras Update, http://www.io.com/~patrik/chupa3.htm.

Clark, Jerome. *Unnatural Phenomena*. Santa Barbara: ABC-CLIO, 2005.

Clark, Jerome, and Loren Coleman. *Creatures of the Outer Edge.* New York: Warner, 1978.

"Club-wielding chimp disappears after sighting." *Ventura County Star*, July 24, 2006.

Coghlan, Ronan. *Cryptosup.* Bangor, No. Ireland: Xiphos, 2005.

—. *A Dictionary of Cryptozoology.* Bangor, No. Ireland: Xiphos, 2004.

—. *Further Cryptozoology.* Bangor, No. Ireland: Xiphos, 2007.

Coleman, Jerry. *More Strange Highways.* Decatur, IL: Whitechapel, 2006.

Coleman, Loren. *Bigfoot!* New York: Paraview, 2003.

—. *Mothman and Other Curious Encounters.* New York: Paraview, 2002.

—. *Mysterious America.* New York: Paraview, 2001.

—. *Tom Slick and the Search for the Yeti.* Boston: Faber and Faber, 1989.

Conant, Roger, and Joseph Collins. *A Field Guide to Reptiles & Amphibians: Eastern-Central North America.* Boston: Houghton Mifflin, 1998.

Cote, John. "'Gorilla' sighted on the peninsula." *San Francisco Chronicle*, Feb. 27, 2007.

Covarrubias, Amanda. "Tiger shot and killed near Reagan Library." *Los Angeles Times*, Feb. 23, 2005.

Daegling, David. *Bigfoot Exposed: An Anthropologist Examines America's Enduring Legend.* Lanham, MD: Altamira Press, 2004.

Dager, Wendy. "Over decades, ongoing tales of the Billiwhack Monster of Santa Paula cast long shadows of doubt." *Ventura County Star,* Oct. 31, 2008.

Dubious Globsters, http://www.geocities.com/caped revenger/dubiousglobsters.html.

Dunn, Geoffrey. "Recently washed-up whale reminds of old legend." *Santa Cruz Sentinel*, Oct. 10, 2004.

Eberhart, George. *Mysterious Creatures.* Santa Barbara: ABC-CLIO, 2002.

"Eight-legged fish barks like dog." *Modesto News*, May 22, 1912.

Ellis, Richard. *The Search for the Giant Squid.* New York: Penguin, 1998.

"Firefighters capture alligator in Wilmington." Los Angeles Fire Department Media & Public Relations, Sept. 9, 2005.

"Fishermen have battle with sea serpent." *Fort Wayne* [IN] *Journal-Gazette*, Feb. 21, 1909.

Gargas, Jane. "Bigfoot as big lie—is someone monkeying around?" *Yakima* (WA) *Herald-Republic*, March 9, 2004.

Garner, Betty. *Monster! Monster!* Blaine, WA: Hancock House, 1995.

"Gator captured." XETV, Channel 6 (San Diego, CA), Dec. 22, 2005.

"Gator surfaces in Lake Machado: Is it Reggie?" KNBC-TV, Channel 4 (Los Angeles), April 30, 2007.

"Giant waterfall discovered in California." CNN News, Aug. 12, 2005.

Green, John. *On the Track of the Sasquatch.* New York: Ballantine, 1973.

—. *Sasquatch: The Apes Among Us.* Blaine, WA: Hancock House, 1978.

Gregor, Ian. "Wranglers nab LA's elusive urban alligator." *Tampa* (FL) *Tribune*, Sept. 13, 2005.

Gresko, Jessica. "Rustlers are hired to net rogue gator." *Los Angeles Times,* Aug. 18, 2005.

Griggs, Gregory. "Mystery cat prowling hills of Simi." *Los Angeles Times*, Feb. 19, 2005.

Guenette, Robert, and Frances Guenette. *The Mysterious Monsters.* Los Angeles: Schick Sun, 1975.

Guiley, Rosemary. *Atlas of the Mysterious in North America.* New York: Facts on File, 1995.

Gulf Coast Bigfoot Research Organization, http://www.gcbro.com.

Hall, Mark. *Thunderbirds.* New York: Paraview, 2004.

Hernandez, Marjorie. "Big cat has crossed Hwy. 23." *Ventura County Star,* Feb. 20, 2005.

Heuvelmans, Bernard. *In the Wake of the Sea Serpents.* New York: Hill & Wang, 1968.

Holder, Charles. *Fish Stories Alleged and Experienced.* New York: Henry Holt, 1909.

Hunter, Carol. "N. Marin farmer shocked by 4-foot lizard." *Marin Independent Journal,* July 10, 2003.

Hunter, Don, and René Dahinden. *Sasquatch.* New York: Signet, 1973.

International Bigfoot Society, http://www.internationalbigfootsociety.com.

"Is Bigfoot living in the forest above Marysville?" CBS 13 (Sacramento, CA): Feb. 26, 2007.

"Is there still a sea serpent of Bolinas?" KGO-TV, Channel 7 (San Francisco), Aug. 4, 2006.

Keel, John. *The Complete Guide to Mysterious Beings.* New York: Doubleday, 1994.

Kirk, John. *In the Domain of the Lake Monsters.* Toronto: Key Porter, 1998.

Kovner, Guy. "Black cougar, or cat, prowls near Forestville." *Press Democrat* (Mendocino, CA), May 2, 2008.

Krantz, Grover. *Bigfoot Sasquatch Evidence.* Blaine, WA: Hancock House, 1999.

Krier, Rob. "It's Lake Hodges—not late-night TV—where you likely may find a monster." *San Diego Union-Tribune,* May 15, 2005.

Krieger, Lisa, and Linda Goldston. "Mystery bird from Africa graces Los Altos Hills." *San Jose Mercury News*, Nov. 29, 2006.

"L.A.: Report of Gator Capture Is Hoax." ABC News, Sept. 13, 2005.

"L.A.'s Reggie the alligator captured, taken to zoo." Fox News, May 29, 2007.

The Lake Hodges Monster, http://www.hodgee.com.

LeBlond, Paul, and Edward Bousfield. *Cadborosaurus.* Victoria, BC: Horsdal & Schubart, 1995.

Lewis, Mike, and Tim Reid. "Hollywood admits to Bigfoot Hoax." *Sunday Telegraph* (London), Oct. 19, 1997.

Littlejohn, Donna. "Chalk up another one for the Machado Lake alligator." *Daily Breeze* (Torrance, CA), Aug. 24, 2005.

—. "City and wranglers plan to let pesky alligator 'chill out.'" *Daily Breeze,* Aug. 19, 2005.

—. "Gator watch day V." *Daily Breeze* (Torrance, CA), Aug. 16, 2005.

—. "Is there room enough in Harbor City for 2 reptiles?" *Daily Breeze,* Sept. 7, 2005.

—. "It's gator vu all over again." *Daily Breeze,* Oct. 1, 2005.

—. "Machado Lake closes after 'alligator' reports prove true." *Daily Breeze,* Aug. 13, 2005.

—. "Officials say they'll 'wait out' harbor park's pesky gator." *Daily Breeze,* Aug. 21, 2005.

Long, Greg. *The Making of Bigfoot.* Amherst, NY: Prometheus, 2004.

Mackey, Brandon. "Big cat loose near Reagan Library." *Ventura County Star*, Feb. 18, 2005.

Malcolm, Andrew. "Somebody's In Over Their Head Here." *Los Angeles Times,* Aug. 19, 2005.

Martin, Glen. "Charlatan in a monkey suit?" *San Francisco Chronicle*, Sept. 14, 2003.

Martinez, Michael. "Elusive gator in L.A. lake has city asking, 'Where's Reggie?'" *Chicago Tribune*, June 14, 2006.

Meldrum, Jeff. *Sasquatch: Legend Meets Science.* New York: Forge, 2006.

"'Monkey-faced owl' raises a ruckus at chicken coop." *Santa Clarita Signal*. Oct. 31, 2004.

"The 'monster' of Loch Chabot." *Contra Costa Times*, July 11, 2002.

Murphy, Christopher. *Bigfoot Encounters in Ohio.* Blaine, WA: Hancock House, 2006.

Murphy, Christopher, and Roger Patterson, *The Bigfoot Film Controversy.* Blaine, WA: Hancock House, 2005.

Myers, George. "Asiatic giant salamander caught in the Sacramento River." *Copeia* 2 (June 1951).

Napier, John. *Bigfoot.* New York: E.P. Dutton, 1972.

"News from around Southern California." *San Jose Mercury News*, Sept. 13, 2004.

Newton, Michael. *Encyclopedia of Cryptozoology.* Jefferson, NC: McFarland, 2005.

Norman, Eric. *The Abominable Snowmen.* New York: Award, 1969.

"On this date: Fishermen spot unknown sea creature." *San Bernardino* (CA) *Sun*, Dec. 4, 2005.

Phillips, Wendy. "Fisherman claims he's seen caiman prowl Lake Chabot." *Oakland Tribune,* July 5, 2002.

"Police arrest two in California on suspicion of putting gator in city lake." WBNS-TV, Channel 10 (Columbus, OH), Aug. 24, 2005.

Pool, Bob. "Reggie the alligator reappears in L.A. lake." *Los Angeles Times*, May 1, 2007.

Powers, Ashley. "Hunting the Monster of Machado Lake." *Los Angeles Times,* Aug. 15, 2005.

—. "It came from the deep." *Los Angeles Times*, May 3, 2005.

Pringle, Paul. "Lion or tiger, not bear, oh my!" *Los Angeles Times,* Feb. 20, 2005.

"Reports of tiger sighting leads to fruitless search." *San Diego Union-Tribune,* Feb. 11, 2006.

Rocha, Guy. "Getting to the bottom of Lake Tahoe." Nevada State Library and Archives, http://dmla.clan.lib.nv. us/docs/nsla/archives/myth/myth151.htm.

Rodgers, Thomas. "Report of giant salamander in California." *Copeia* 3 (September 1962).

Sanderson, Ivan. *Abominable Snowmen: Legend Come to Life.* Philadelphia: Chilton, 1961.

—. *More "Things."* New York: Pyramid, 1969.

Santschi, Darrell. "Wild parrots ruffle feathers in Redlands." *Riverside Press-Enterprise*, Nov. 25, 2006.

Schoch, Deborah. "An odd lizard lives in huge numbers nearby." *Los Angeles Times*, Dec. 30, 2003.

"The SCV's most famous no-show." *The Signal* (Santa Clara, CA), Dec. 28, 2006.

Sheffield, Keith. "Dark shapes in the lake." *Tahoe Daily Tribune*, April 29, 2005.

—. "Tessie pops up for an afternoon appearance." *Tahoe World*, April 27, 2005.

Shuker, Karl. *In Search of Prehistoric Survivors*. London: Blandford, 1995.

—. *Mystery Cats of the World*. London: Robert Hale, 1989.

Slate, Ann, and Alan Berry. *Bigfoot*. New York: Bantam, 1976.

"SoCal town collars strange critter—a wallaby." *San Jose Mercury News*, Feb. 6, 2007.

Spiewak, Sam. "Woodworker summons the sea serpent." *Point Reyes Light*, Sept. 5, 2006.

Stanley, Robert. "Lost land of the lizard people." The Reptilian Agenda, http://www.reptilianagenda.com/ research/r110199k.shtml.

Stebbins, Robert. *A Field Guide to Western Reptiles and Amphibians*. Boston: Houghton Mifflin, 1985.

Stienstra, Tom. "'Black panther sightings' in Bay Area parks." *San Francisco Chronicle*, Nov. 13, 2008.

—. "Hills are alive with sound of rumors." *San Francisco Chronicle*, Nov. 7, 2004.

—. "Mysteries of the deep at Lake Tahoe." *San Francisco Chronicle*, July 25, 2004.

—. "The mysterious black panther makes a rare appearance, scout reports." *San Francisco Chronicle*, April 13, 2008.

Stinnett, Peggy. "'Creature' discovered in Lake Merritt." *Oakland Tribune*, Dec. 31, 2003.

"'Stressed' gator makes Calif. lake home." *Washington Post,* Aug. 19, 2005.

"Support Your Local Reptoid." *Skeptoid* 46 (May 21, 2007), http://skeptoid.com/episodes/4046.

"Suspected lion tracked near Reagan Library." *San Jose Mercury News*, Feb. 19, 2005.

"Tales of Tahoe lake monster just story?" KRON-TV, Channel 4 (San Francisco), Jan. 28, 2004.

Tapia, Catherine. "Lake Hodges monster returns—and now it's doing PR." *San Diego Citybeat,* Dec. 17, 2003.

Thermos, Wendy. "Wrangler may have met his match in Reggie." *Los Angeles Times*, Aug. 29, 2005.

"Tiger spotted in Valley Center." NBC San Diego, Channel 7, Feb. 13, 2006.

"Time Past: 1934—A monster lurks in Lake Elsinore."
Los Angeles Times, Sept. 13, 2006.

"Trucker reports bigfoot sighting." *Curry Coastal Pilot* (Brookings, OR), Sept. 24, 2005.

Unger, Rebecca. "OK, so it's not a chupacabra." *Hi-Desert Star* (Yucca Valley, CA), Aug. 6, 2008.

Walton, Bruce. Mount Shasta: Home of the Ancients. Mokelumne Hill, CS: Health Research, 1986.

Wasson, David. "Bigfoot unzipped: Man claims it was him in a suit." *Yakima* (WA) *Herald-Republic,* Jan. 30, 1999.

Weird California, http://www.weirdca.com.

Wides, Laura. "Tiger shot, killed near Reagan library." *Grand Forks* (ND) *Herald*, Feb. 23, 2005.

"The wild man—what is he?" *Petersburg* (VA) *Index,* April 29, 1871.
"The wild men of California." *Titusville* (PA) *Morning Herald,* Nov. 10, 1870.

Young, Bob. "Lovable trickster created a monster with Bigfoot hoax." *Seattle Times,* Dec. 5, 2002.

Zieralski, Ed. "Lower Otay Lake's lizard is busy livin' large." *San Diego Union-Tribune*, Feb. 5, 2006.

Monster Index